IT HAPPENED IN
NEW MEXICO

IT HAPPENED IN
NEW MEXICO

**Stories of Events and People that
Shaped the LAND OF ENCHANTMENT**

Third Edition

JAMES A.
CRUTCHFIELD

Globe
Pequot   ESSEX, CONNECTICUT

Globe Pequot

An imprint of Globe Pequot, the trade division of
The Rowman & Littlefield Publishing Group, Inc.
4501 Forbes Blvd., Ste. 200
Lanham, MD 20706
www.rowman.com

Distributed by NATIONAL BOOK NETWORK

British Library Cataloguing in Publication Information available

Library of Congress Cataloging-in-Publication Data
Names: Crutchfield, James A., 1938– author.
Title: It happened in New Mexico : stories of events and people that shaped the
    Land of Enchantment / James A. Crutchfield.
Description: Third edition. | Lanham, MD : Globe Pequot, [2023] | Includes
    bibliographical references and index. | Summary: "Fascinating stories about
    thirty-three events that helped make New Mexico what it is today. Read about
    Pancho Villa, Charles Bent, Smokey the Bear, and many more, including
    little-known episodes that shaped New Mexico's colorful history"—Provided
    by publisher.
Identifiers: LCCN 2022040837 (print) | LCCN 2022040838 (ebook) | ISBN
    9781493070404 (paperback) | ISBN 9781493070411 (epub)
Subjects: LCSH: New Mexico—History—Anecdotes.
Classification: LCC F796.6 .C78 2023 (print) | LCC F796.6 (ebook) | DDC
    972—dc23/eng/20220831
LC record available at https://lccn.loc.gov/2022040837
LC ebook record available at https://lccn.loc.gov/2022040838

♾™ The paper used in this publication meets the minimum requirements of
American National Standard for Information Sciences—Permanence of Paper
for Printed Library Materials, ANSI/NISO Z39.48-1992.

*To Alice and Bill and Alice, who first
showed us the pleasures of New Mexico*

CONTENTS

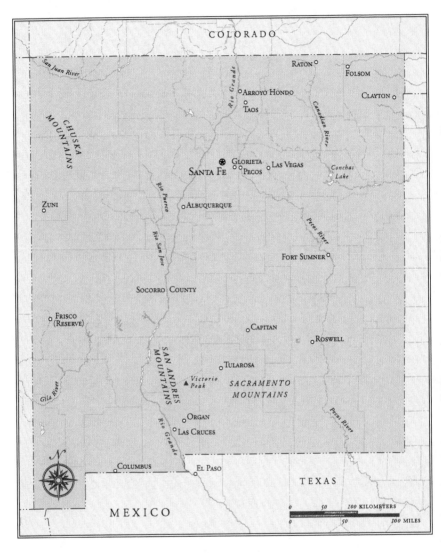

COLORADO

San Juan River

RATON ○

FOLSOM ○

Rio Grande

ARROYO HONDO ○

TAOS ○

CLAYTON ○

CHUSKA MOUNTAINS

Canadian River

⊗ GLORIETA
SANTA FE ○ PECOS ○ LAS VEGAS ○

Conchas Lake

ZUNI ○

Rio Puerco

ALBUQUERQUE ○

Rio San Jose

Pecos River

FORT SUMNER ○

SOCORRO COUNTY

FRISCO (RESERVE) ○

CAPITAN ○

ROSWELL ○

SAN ANDRES MOUNTAINS

TULAROSA ○

Gila River

▲ *Victorio Peak*

SACRAMENTO MOUNTAINS

Pecos River

ORGAN ○
LAS CRUCES ○

Rio Grande

N

COLUMBUS ○

EL PASO ○

TEXAS

MEXICO

0   50   100 KILOMETERS
0   50   100 MILES

NEW MEXICO

PREFACE

This book highlights several interesting episodes of New Mexico history, from the days of the prehistoric Native Americans through modern times. Each story is complete in itself and can be read individually and out of sequence.

New Mexico is an extremely important state historically, and although the vignettes related in this book do not in any way purport to be a thorough history of the state, they have been chosen selectively to give the reader a broad understanding of the varied history of the "Land of Enchantment."

I hope that *It Happened in New Mexico* will provide a few hours of pleasure to those who read it, and that it will, perhaps find its way into the classrooms of the state, thereby giving younger generations a better appreciation of their vast heritage.

9,000 BC

The Life and Times of Folsom Man

On a cloudless, late summer's day about eleven thousand years ago, a group of Paleo-Native Americans squatted around a cooking fire burning in a tiny pit dug out of the prairie soil. The small band, numbering no more than half a dozen men, as many women, and ten or twelve youngsters, watched intently as one of the men, the leader, put the finishing touches on a finely flaked spear blade he had just fashioned from a naturally occurring flint nodule. The man held the point high above his head and with a broad smile declared that this was the weapon that today would bring the hungry band good luck. All heads nodded in agreement as the artisan tied the long, fluted point to the end of a wooden shaft several feet long. When he had finished the task, he waved the spear back and forth through the air as if plunging it into the side of some great animal.

One of the women kicked the dying embers of the fire, and the band of people picked up their sparse belongings and headed southwest across the prairie. In the distance they could see the brooding cone of a small volcano, Capulin, located in the northwest corner of today's Union County, New Mexico. Some of the group had been told that their grandfathers' grandfathers had seen the mountain belch forth fire and burning rocks at some distant time in the past, but no one among them could remember such an occurrence. Perhaps the ever-present wisps of dark, foul-smelling smoke spewing from the mountain's uppermost heights were a warning that such an eruption could again take place sometime in the future.

When the Paleo-tribesmen had traveled just a few miles, they came across a giant bison, a member of a species that grew to a much larger size than the familiar buffalo of today. Two of the men went on ahead to observe the strange antics of the bison and soon learned that the animal had been hurt and was struggling to stay on all four legs. Here, at last, they thought, were the makings of a gigantic feast that would feed the hunters and their families for several days.

The six men in the party carefully surrounded the wounded beast, which was not only in intense pain from wounds suffered in a recent wolf attack but was now bewildered and frightened by the abrupt appearance of so many hunters. Each of the men held his spear high above his head and carefully sallied back and forth just out of the bison's reach. While the terrified animal fought off three men at his front, one of the hunters, the one who had fashioned his fluted spear point that very morning, approached from the side and thrust his long weapon deep into the bison's rib cage. Bellowing with pain, the bison turned in circles, attempting to fight off its enemies.

One by one the hunters shoved their flint-tipped spears into the doomed bison's side. Within a few moments the magnificent animal was dead, and the women and children ran up to the massive hulk of flesh and began to skin and dismember the body. All that could be heard around the campfire that night were stories about the strength and bravery of the man who had made the flint blade and who, with his brand-new weapon, had delivered the first blow to the bison that was now being prepared for the evening's supper.

After staying in the vicinity of the bison kill for a couple of days, the people picked up their few belongings and moved across the prairie to another camp several miles away. Day after day the sun's hot rays pounded down upon what little of the bison's flesh and bones remained after the wolves and vultures had found it. In time the only vestige of the animal's body was a ghostly white skeleton bleaching upon the hard-packed earth. Eventually, layer after layer of soil covered the remains.

For thousands of years the skeleton of the once powerful beast lay undisturbed beneath the surface of the earth. More centuries passed, and rain, more plentiful in prehistoric days than it is now, pounded the region and carved a tiny gully. In time, as the arroyo grew deeper and deeper, the ancient bison's bones were once again exposed.

Eleven thousand years later, in 1908, a black cowboy named George McJunkin was riding herd for his boss on the Crowfoot Ranch in eastern New Mexico. It had been raining hard for several days, and the area that McJunkin was visiting had several arroyos etched across its face. McJunkin noticed that one of these gulches, known locally as Wild Horse Arroyo, appeared to be several feet deeper than it had been the last time he had ridden this part of the range. The curious cowboy decided to investigate.

As McJunkin neared the edge of Wild Horse Arroyo, then ten feet deep, he saw a white, glistening object protruding from the side of the gully. Dismounting, he eased himself down into the arroyo and examined it. It was a large bone of an animal that McJunkin decided was a huge species of bison. The cowboy dug the bone out of the dirt, wrapped it in a slicker, and carried it home.

Nineteen years later, six months after McJunkin's death, Carl Schwachheim, a local blacksmith and amateur "bone hunter," rode out to Wild Horse Arroyo and dug around in the earth of this gulch that his friend McJunkin had so often told him about. Almost immediately Schwachheim found a pair of bison ribs with a fluted spear point imbedded in them. He was quick to realize that his find meant that man was present at the time the bison was killed.

As news of the blacksmith's find spread to the scientific community, archaeologists and anthropologists from all over the United States descended upon the little town of Folsom, New Mexico, the village nearest to the site. Within weeks the scientists were declaring that the bison and spear point found at the "Folsom" site proved that people had been present in North America at least eleven thousand years ago, since the giant bison became extinct shortly after that time. A whole new phase of American history was defined by that simple discovery made by George McJunkin and Carl Schwachheim on the Crowfoot Ranch.

In addition to Folsom Man, New Mexico has been home to other ancient finds that date as far back as 12,000 B.C.

Spear points, along with extinct animal species, were found near the small town of Clovis, New Mexico, in 1933. These discoveries place New Mexico in the unique position of having been the site of some of the oldest and most important prehistoric Native American artifacts yet discovered in North America.

AD 1540

Cibola Falls to the Spanish

The Spanish conquistador Francisco Vásquez de Coronado, along with several hundred soldiers and friendly Natives, had just reached the village of Hawikuh in the province of Cibola. The province was reported to be full of treasure, and its "seven cities of gold," which another Spaniard, Fray Marcos, had reportedly visited the previous year, were described as "larger than the city of Mexico." Marcos had written that Cibola was a fabulously rich region with "a great store of gold . . . and a hill of silver."

Coronado and his entourage had left Compostela, far to the south in Mexico, 134 days earlier. Now, in the blistering heat of July 7, 1540, as he searched the distant horizon for signs of the golden riches Marcos had described, Coronado suddenly reached the bitter conclusion that Marcos had either been misinformed or was a monumental liar. Instead of a town whose inhabitants "wear silk clothing down to their feet" and that contained "a temple of their idols, the walls of which were covered with precious stones," as Marcos had reported, Coronado had found nothing but a dusty pueblo inhabited by several hundred hostile warriors anxiously perched on the roofs of their adobe houses. The village was near today's settlement of Zuni, about thirty-three miles south of Gallup, New Mexico.

Coronado's Spanish and Native troops were tired and hungry. As they approached Hawikuh, one of the soldiers rode ahead with an interpreter and a priest and ordered the pueblo inhabitants to submit to the Spanish crown and the Catholic Church. His demand was met by Zuni defenders with derisive yells, gestures, and an arrow that almost made a martyr of the priest. Realizing that a peaceful entry into the village was out of the question, Coronado gave the order to attack.

After two sorties, in which several soldiers, including twenty-six-year-old Coronado, were wounded, the conquistadors took the town and its supposed treasure. Hundreds of terrified Zunis fled to neighboring villages. Coronado later wrote that:

> [the natives of Hawikuh] all directed their attack against me because my armor was gilded and glittered and on this account I was hurt more than the rest, and not because I had done more or was farther in advance than the others; for all these gentlemen and soldiers bore themselves well, as was expected of them.

Pedro de Castaneda, a chronicler traveling with Coronado's party, confirmed in his journal that the attack on Hawikuh was difficult and described his leader's mishap in battle.

During the attack they knocked the general down with a large stone, and would have killed him but for Don Garcia Lopez de Cardenas and Hernando de Alvarado, who threw themselves above him and drew him away, receiving the blows of the stones, which were not few.

After taking the town, Coronado's men fell upon the food stores like hungry animals. Rummaging through the defeated village, the soldiers "found that of which there was greater need than of gold or silver, which was much corn, and beans, and fowl better than those of New Spain, and salt, the best and whitest I have seen in all my life," according to one eyewitness. After gorging themselves on the spoils of war, Coronado and his officers discussed their bearings and laid plans for the future. A dozen horsemen under the command of Cardenas were sent westward in search of a great river that was rumored to exist far away in the land of the Hopis. Departing what they thought was Cibola in late August, Cardenas and his followers soon came upon the magnificent Grand Canyon of the Colorado River at some unknown point on its south rim, thus becoming the first known European men to view the natural wonder.

In the meantime, Coronado decided to send another party eastward in search of other cities that might prove more rewarding than Hawikuh. Alvarado led a group that left Hawikuh in late August. Some weeks later he sent a message back to Coronado, recommending that winter camp be pitched near the site of today's city of Bernalillo, New

Mexico. Pushing eastward, Alvarado entered the village of "Cicuye," later known as Pecos Pueblo. Castaneda, the chronicler, described the town as:

> a pueblo containing 500 warriors. It is feared throughout the land. It is square, perched on a rock in the center of a vast patio or plaza. . . . The houses are all alike, four stories high. One can walk on the roofs over the whole pueblo, there being no streets to prevent this. . . . The houses have no doors on the ground floor. The inhabitants use movable ladders to climb the corridors which are on the inner side of the pueblos. They enter them that way, as the doors of the houses open into the corridors on this terrace. . . . The pueblo is surrounded by a low stone wall. Inside there is a water spring, which can be diverted from them. The people of this town pride themselves because no one had been able to subjugate them, while they dominate the pueblos as they wish.

In addition to being awed by the majesty of Pecos, Alvarado was also intrigued by a story its people told him. Far to the east, they said, beyond the great prairies where the buffalo were as numerous as insects in the summertime, lay a magical kingdom known as Quivira, which was full of the riches for which the conquistadors had traveled so far. When Alvarado reported this marvelous tale to Coronado, the Spanish army made immediate plans to move eastward. Shortly after visiting Pecos himself, in the spring of 1541, Coronado led his weary forces out of New Mexico and onto the vast and lonely Great Plains.

The Pueblo Natives of New Mexico had tasted the steel of the conquistadors and heard the promises of the Catholic

Church. Coronado's battle at Hawikuh was the first known armed conflict between Europeans and Native Americans in the territory that one day would become the United States. But it would not be the last.

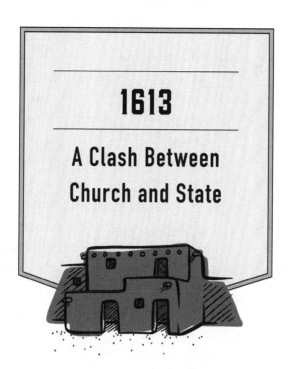

1613

A Clash Between Church and State

On Tuesday morning, July 9, 1613, in the three-year-old village of Santa Fe, the royal governor of New Mexico, Pedro de Peralta, assembled several of his lieutenants and ordered them to prepare for a dangerous confrontation. The governor told the soldiers that they were to accompany him across the plaza to the Franciscan church, where he intended to order the friar Isidro Ordonez, out of town.

Peralta, decked out in a suit of chain mail and armed with a sword and pistol, led the men toward the church. As Mass ended, Ordonez approached Peralta wielding a wooden cane. Ordering his companions to search the church for weapons, Peralta demanded that the priest leave Santa Fe and return to Santo Domingo Pueblo, which served as the ecclesiastical headquarters of the Catholic

Church in northern New Mexico. The priest refused to budge and attempted to strike Peralta with his cane. The governor drew his pistol, and when someone in the tightly packed church grabbed his arm, he accidentally shot and wounded an onlooking priest.

The gunfire dispersed the crowd, but the angry Ordonez promptly excommunicated Peralta and a few of his men. Then he left Santa Fe for Santo Domingo to confer with other churchmen about how to depose the governor.

Peralta had moved the seat of government from San Gabriel a few miles south to Santa Fe in 1610. For the first two years in the new town, affairs had gone well. The governor had laid out the village to include residences, public buildings, and the structure that would soon become known as the Palace of the Governors. Councilmen were elected, judges were appointed, and residents were given the opportunity to acquire, free of charge, "two lots for house and garden, two contiguous fields for vegetable gardens, two others for vineyards and olive groves" in addition to 133 acres of rural land for farming. Water was guaranteed. The only requirement was that the resident must live on the property for ten consecutive years.

Trouble began when Ordonez illegally relieved the previous priest in Santa Fe of his church duties and wrangled the assignment for himself. An extremely zealous but hard-hearted man, Ordonez set to work to undermine the civil authority of Governor Peralta, who exclaimed when he received the news of the priest's assignment to Santa Fe, "Would to God the devil were coming instead of that friar!" In May 1613, when Peralta confronted Ordonez over who had authority over tribute collectors, the growing rift between the two headstrong men became irreparable.

On a bright Sunday in July, when Peralta entered church for Mass, he found that the chair that was always reserved for him was missing. It was clear that his nemesis had ordered the chair thrown into the yard. Peralta retrieved the chair, placed it in the back of the church among the Natives, and sat down. The priest's sermon was obviously for his benefit.

Do not be deceived. Let no one persuade himself with vain words that I do not have the same power and authority that the Pope in Rome has, or that if his Holiness were here in New Mexico he could do more than I. Believe you that I can arrest, cast into irons, and punish as seems fitting to me any person without exception who is not obedient to the commandments of the church and mine. What I have told you, I say for the benefit of a certain person who is listening to me who perhaps raises his eyebrows.

After the July 9 confrontation between Peralta and Ordonez, and after Ordonez had returned from his conference with his associates in Santo Domingo, the governor decided that he would personally travel to Mexico City and present his case against the aberrant priest. Since he knew that Ordonez's men kept a constant watch on his quarters, Peralta bided his time, finally slipping out of Santa Fe and heading south. However, Ordonez's followers caught up with him at Isleta Pueblo, south of Albuquerque, and arrested him.

The governor was sent in chains to the mission at Sandia, where he was incarcerated for nine months. During Peralta's absence, Ordonez ruled both religious and civil affairs in Santa Fe with an iron fist. "Excommunications were rained down . . . and because of the terrors that walked abroad the people were not only scandalized but afraid. . . . [E]xistence in the villa was a hell," wrote one witness to the events.

A new governor, Bernardino de Ceballos, was appointed to fill Peralta's office in Santa Fe. At first he vowed to obtain the former governor's release from prison and let him return to private life, but he gradually forgot his promise. Peralta was eventually freed, and he left New Mexico penniless. When he arrived in Mexico City in 1615, he told his superiors about affairs in the north.

In 1615, church authorities found ample reason to question Fray Ordonez's handling of affairs in New Mexico. However, two years passed before the matter came to a head. In 1617 the wayward priest was finally summoned to Mexico City, where he was rebuked and replaced. Church and state continued to clash in New Mexico for years to come, although not always as dramatically as during the days of Ordonez and Peralta.

1680

The Pueblo Revolt

At his headquarters in Taos Pueblo, about sixty-two miles north of the Spanish capital at Santa Fe, the Tewa medicine man Popé spoke in hushed tones. His listeners were representatives of the two dozen or so pueblo towns that stretched up and down the Rio Grande and as far west as today's Arizona border. Although not a native of Taos, Popé had been given refuge there when it became too dangerous for him to stay at his own pueblo of San Juan, several miles to the southwest. Popé was a hunted man, and his whereabouts were always of interest to Spanish authorities, with whom he seemed continually to be at odds. Five years earlier he had been arrested, accused of witchcraft, and flogged by henchmen of Governor Juan Francisco de Trevino in Santa Fe. And Popé's feelings for the Spanish were mutual!

It was early August 1680, and Popé and some of the Pueblo Natives were meeting at Taos Pueblo to put the finishing touches on plans for an uprising against the Spanish by most of the Pueblo peoples living in northern New Mexico. As Popé surveyed the crowd sitting against the walls of the small, dark room, he stressed the importance of secrecy. No women were allowed at the meeting. Popé even had his own brother-in-law executed when he suspected him of leaking the plan.

This was to be the final meeting of the conspirators before the uprising on August 11. After last-minute preparations had been made, the men in the room rose to depart. But one last item of business needed to be addressed before the group disbanded. Popé handed each participant a short rope with a number of knots tied in it. This rope, he explained, was the timetable for the rebellion. Each day the rope's caretaker was to untie one knot. When the last one was undone, that was the day when the Pueblos would rise up and destroy their Spanish masters.

As it turned out, someone leaked the secret after all. Popé, to keep momentum going, declared that the revolt would take place one day earlier than planned. And so it was that on August 10, 1680, nearly seventeen thousand Pueblo Natives—who, although similar to one another in culture and lifestyle, spoke six different languages—arose as one people and attacked the Spanish settlements along the Rio Grande.

Scores of Spanish farmers and ranchers were killed, and those who did survive the initial onslaught fled to Santa Fe or to Isleta Pueblo, whose inhabitants had not participated in the uprising. Santa Fe, whose one thousand Spanish citizens were protected by only about one hundred armed men under the command of the new Governor Antonio de Otermi, was surrounded by two thousand Natives. On August 21, the hungry and thirsty Spanish at Santa Fe ended the siege by surrendering the town to the rebels and retreating southward to El Paso.

The Pueblo Revolt of 1680 left terrible carnage. Of about twenty-five hundred Spaniards living in New Mexico at the time, at least four hundred had been killed. Farms and ranches had been destroyed. Churches, government buildings, and houses had been burned to the ground as the Pueblos attempted to reclaim their homeland.

Popé, it seems, had been especially intent upon purging all Christian influences. According to one of his lieutenants, captured later by Spanish authorities, Popé commanded that his followers

> break up and burn the images of the holy Christ, the virgin Mary and the other saints, the crosses, and everything pertaining to Christianity, and that they burn the temples, break up the bells, and separate from the wives whom God had given them in marriage and take those whom they desired. In order to take away their baptismal names, the water, and the holy oils, they were to plunge into the rivers and wash themselves. . . . [T]here would thus be taken from them the character of holy sacraments.

For the next ten years, most of the Spanish refugees from New Mexico lived in exile in El Paso. By 1690, however, Popé had died, and the following year, a new Spanish governor, Diego de Vargas, arrived from Madrid to assume responsibility for the northern provinces. In 1692, after visiting several of the Pueblo towns that had rebelled, Vargas perceived that the time was right to reassert Spanish authority. However, the pompous governor was a little premature when he carved the following memorial on Inscription Rock: "Here was the General Don Diego de Vargas, who conquered for our Holy Faith, and for the Royal Crown, all the New Mexico, at his expense, Year of 1692."

Actually, it took the governor until 1694 to subdue some of the more recalcitrant Pueblo Natives, who had not yet forgotten what it was like to live under the yoke of Spanish oppression.

1776

The Dominguez–
Escalante Expedition

On July 29, 1776, less than a month after the Declaration of Independence was signed in faraway Philadelphia, ten men gathered in the plaza opposite the governor's palace in Santa Fe. The group was about to begin a journey that its leaders hoped would take it to Monterey, California, and back again. The explorers left Santa Fe peacefully, "without noise of arms," and with the hope that "God will facilitate our passage as far as befits His honor, glory, and the fulfillment of the will of the All High that all men be saved." Although it fell short of its goal to reach California, the expedition traveled more than two thousand miles across the wilderness that is today Colorado, Utah, Arizona, and New Mexico before returning to Santa Fe on January 2, 1777.

The two leaders of the expedition were Francisco Atanasio Dominguez, a thirty-six-year-old Franciscan missionary, and Silvestre Velez de Escalante, a Franciscan friar about ten years younger. For several months prior to the journey, Escalante had been a missionary at both Laguna Pueblo and at Zuni. Dominguez had also visited among various Pueblo tribes, having been sent by his superiors in Mexico City to inspect and document the lands of northern New Spain.

It was an odd assemblage that left Santa Fe that July morning. Accompanying the two Franciscan friars were an astronomer/cartographer, a chief guide and interpreter, a magistrate from Zuni, a blacksmith, and four others. In addition to the horses they rode, the group took extra mounts, pack mules, and cattle. The expedition headed north and soon passed Tesuque Pueblo, a Tewa-speaking village just a few miles away. Tracing very closely the route that U.S. Highway 84/285 follows today, the adventurers passed but did not stop at neighboring Pojoaque and Nambé Pueblos, also Tewa-speaking villages. Near San Ildefonso Pueblo, they spotted the hallowed Black Mesa—La Mesilla, as Dominguez called it—and although the men were anxious to get to Santa Clara Pueblo to prepare the first night's camp, the expedition cartographer, Bernardo de Miera y Pacheco, took the time to plot the plateau's position on his map. Even today this 550-foot-high mesa is sacred ground to the several tribes of Tewa-speaking Pueblo Natives who dwell in the region.

Crossing the Rio del Norte (today's Rio Grande) to Santa Clara Pueblo, the ten explorers spent the first of many nights under the brilliant stars that dotted the pitch-black southwestern skies.

Santa Clara was well-known to the members of the expedition because it was so near Santa Fe. Nevertheless, the mapmaker, de Miera, took the time to describe the village in his journal. He wrote that "all the houses [have] portable ladders which they pull up in time of invasion . . . the roofs and upper and lower terraces with embrasures in the parapets for defense against the enemy." Dominguez, always interested in church affairs, added that the sanctuary at Santa Clara "had very thick walls."

The next day the Dominguez–Escalante expedition followed a "rough road" up the banks of the Rio Chama, more or less tracing today's US 84, to Abiquiu, a small village that represented the northwesternmost reach of Spanish influence in New Spain. This was the last outpost of comfort for the travelers. From then on they would cross uncharted wilderness inhabited by Ute Natives and other tribes they knew little about.

For the next several days, the adventurers traveled generally northwestward. On August 1, they left the banks of the Rio Chama and proceeded through the mountain wilderness that is today Carson National Forest. Near the modern-day town of Canjilon, the men entered a beautiful region described by Dominguez as "a small plain of abundant pasturage which is very pleasing to the sight, because it produces some flowers whose color is between purple and white and which, if they are not carnations, are very much like carnations of that color." Passing the site of today's town of Tierra Amarilla, the men crossed the Continental Divide near Monero. They forded the headwaters of the San Juan River near Carracas and crossed today's New Mexico–Colorado border on August 5.

For the next three and a half months, the explorers traveled through today's states of Colorado, Utah, and Arizona. In early October, while snowbound in the mountains of Utah, they decided they would not attempt to make it all the way to California, fearing that "long before we arrived the passes would be closed and we would be delayed for two or three months in some *sierra*, where there might be no people nor any means of obtaining necessary sustenance."

On November 24, the party crossed the present-day boundary between Arizona and New Mexico. At Zuni Pueblo they rested for seventeen days. Dominguez anticipated the findings of future linguists when he commented that the Zuni people spoke "an entirely different language from all those known and observed in the kingdom." From Zuni the expedition passed El Morro, today's Inscription Rock, upon which the travelers' countryman, Governor Juan de Oñate, had once carved his name.

At Acoma Pueblo the men were delayed when a heavy snowstorm temporarily marooned them on the 357-foot-high mesa. They visited several other pueblos, and at one of them, Isleta, they celebrated Christmas. They entered Albuquerque on December 28. From there they continued northward to Santa Fe, arriving on January 2, 1777. The next day Dominguez and Escalante presented the governor with their diary, which they said was "true and faithful to what happened and as observed in our journey."

Although the expedition failed in its original goal to reach Monterey, its members traveled through regions never before seen by white men and recorded what they saw. They encountered Native American tribes unknown to their superiors back in New Spain. Indeed the two humble friars made a monumental journey of discovery, all the more satisfying because it was a peaceful one and made "without noise of arms."

1807

An American Army Officer in Santa Fe

History has failed to record just how Lieutenant Zebulon Pike expected to be received by Spanish authorities in Santa Fe as he rode into the village in early March 1807. The American army officer was escorted by a company of colorfully uniformed dragoons, each decked out in "a short blue coat, with red cape and cuffs ... and ... a broad brimmed, high crowned wool hat," and armed with a carbine, pistol, and cutlass.

But history has preserved Pike's initial impression of Santa Fe. In his lengthy book about his journey to New Mexico, entitled *An Account of Expeditions to the Sources of the Mississippi, and through the Western Parts of Louisiana*, Pike described the capital of Spain's northernmost province in North America as follows:

Its appearance from a distance struck my mind with the same effect as a fleet of the flat bottomed boats, which are seen in the spring and fall seasons, descending the Ohio River. There are two churches, the magnificence of whose steeples form a striking contrast to the miserable appearance of the houses. On the north side of the town is the square of soldiers houses, equal to 120 or 140 on each flank. The public square is in the center of the town; on the north side of which is situated the palace (as the[y] term it) or government house, with the quarters for guards, &c.

As Pike rode down the narrow, dusty street that led to the palace and the waiting governor, he must have contemplated the events that had brought him to this foreign land. It had all begun on July 15, 1806, when Pike and twenty-three soldiers left Saint Louis under the orders of the governor of Louisiana Territory, General James Wilkinson, ostensibly to explore the headwaters of the Red River. In reality, Wilkinson and his close associate, former U.S. Vice President Aaron Burr, privately nurtured dreams of creating a renegade Spanish-American government in which they would be the kingpins.

It was with this scheme in mind that Wilkinson dispatched Pike to the far West to spy on the territories and towns of northern New Spain. In late February 1807, the Americans crossed the boundary that separated Louisiana from New Spain and were confronted by Spanish soldiers near the headwaters of the Rio Grande. Although they were not officially arrested, Pike and his companions were marched to Santa Fe for an interview with the governor.

Near the Palace of the Governors, Pike was confronted by a crowd of curious onlookers. He was likely the first American that many of them had ever seen. Although his uniform of "blue trowsers, mockinsons, blanket coat and a cap made of scarlet cloth, lined with fox skins," was torn and dirty after months of travel, the young lieutenant still cut a dashing figure. Dismounting at the palace, he was escorted into an anteroom where he awaited the governor's arrival.

Pike's interview with Governor Joaquín del Rael Alencaster did not go well. The lieutenant could tell that the governor was attempting to trap him into admitting that the real goal of his mission was to spy on the inhabitants and facilities of New Spain's northern frontier. In another interview later that evening, Pike tried to assure the governor that he harbored "no hostile intentions toward the Spanish government." After reading Pike's army commission and orders, the governor "gave me his hand, for the first time, and said he was happy to be acquainted with me as a man of honor," Pike later recalled.

The next day, after examining the contents of Pike's trunk and finding incriminating letters, Governor Alencaster informed the American that he must go to Chihuahua to be interviewed by Spanish authorities.

"If we go to Chihuahua we must be considered as prisoners of war," asserted an exasperated Pike.

"By no means," replied Alencaster. "You will dine with me today and march afterwards to a village about six miles distant . . . where the remainder of your escort is now waiting for you."

From that point Pike would begin the long trip to Chihuahua. Before leaving the interview, he was given a shirt and scarf made by the governor's sister "and never worn by any person."

After a dinner at the governor's palace consisting of "a variety of dishes and wines of the southern provinces," Alencaster accompanied Pike to the outskirts of town.

"Remember Alencaster, in peace or war," the governor called out as Pike headed south with the Spanish military escort.

Following the interrogation in Chihuahua, Pike and his men were eventually released. When he returned to the United States, he reported from memory to an anxious General Wilkinson all that he had seen and heard in New Spain. Of course nothing came of Wilkinson's and Burr's southwestern colonization scheme, but as the War of 1812 approached, Pike's star continued to rise in the army and he was progressively promoted through the ranks. By March 1813, he was a brigadier general, and at the Battle of York, Ontario, the following month, he was killed.

Probably more important than the military intelligence Pike brought back with him from New Spain were his comments on the nature and potential uses of the land through which he had passed. He was responsible for the propagation of the "Great American Desert" myth, which discouraged American immigration to the southern Great Plains for years. He wrote in his book that the vast, treeless prairie would restrict "our population to some certain limits," and that

> our citizens being so prone to rambling and extending themselves on the frontiers will, through necessity, be constrained to limit their extent on the west to the borders of the Missouri and Mississippi, while they leave the prairies incapable of cultivation to the wandering and uncivilized aborigines of the country.

1820

A Prisoner in Santa Fe

It was midsummer 1820 when nineteen-year-old David Meriwether searched for a campsite along one of the many tributaries of today's Canadian River in northern New Mexico. With him was a black cook named Alfred and a few Pawnee Natives, led by their chief, Big Elk. Meriwether, born in Virginia and raised in Kentucky, was a distant kinsman of Meriwether Lewis of the Lewis and Clark expedition. Since New Mexico was still under the control of Spain, an archenemy of the United States, Meriwether knew that his trip could be dangerous.

Meriwether was experienced for his age. The previous year he had been hired as a trader and sutler for Colonel Henry Atkinson's Yellowstone Expedition. Following his service with Atkinson on the upper Missouri, during which he met his companion Alfred, Meriwether returned to Council Bluffs, anxious to make a trip to New Mexico to investigate stories of abundant gold there.

As Meriwether looked about the campsite he had selected, he noticed many horse and mule tracks in the sand and mud. Alarmed, he reported the tracks to his Pawnee companions and suggested that they move on and camp elsewhere. But Big Elk studied the stream bank himself and declared that the tracks were old and so their presence posed no danger. Unconvinced, Meriwether and Alfred crossed the stream and pitched their camp in the hills several hundred yards away.

The following morning at dawn, the sound of gunfire awakened Meriwether and Alfred. The Pawnees, who despite Meriwether's apprehensions had spent the night on the riverbank, were under attack. Soon Big Elk and another man rode into Meriwether's camp and told the alarmed American that Mexicans had raided his camp and killed most of the other Pawnees.

Under a flag of truce, Meriwether and Alfred ventured toward the Mexican encampment, where they were disarmed and stripped of all valuables. The following day, after spending "a miserable night," Meriwether and Alfred were marched westward, on foot, by the Mexicans. When Meriwether refused to move on after a rest stop because his feet were sore, he was given a mule to ride.

Several days later the entourage arrived in Santa Fe, where Meriwether was presented to the governor. After a brief audience—the American could speak no Spanish and the governor could speak no English—Meriwether was thrown into a prison cell "with only a small window about the size of a pane of eight by ten glass to admit a little fresh air and light."

After a couple of days of prison life, during which he was harassed by bedbugs and fleas, Meriwether was visited by a French-speaking Mexican priest. Since Meriwether spoke French, he could now complete his interview with the governor. The priest acted as interpreter, and the young American attempted to explain the purpose of his visit to the disbelieving official. Meriwether spent several more days in the squalor of his dark cell before his friend, the priest, visited him again. In another interview with the governor, Meriwether was more or less placed under house arrest. He was free to explore the town in the daytime but obliged to report back to jail at night. Later still the governor freed Meriwether altogether, as long as the priest could account for his whereabouts.

As autumn approached, an old Mexican man hired Meriwether to help harvest peppers and beans from his garden. Then, Meriwether later recalled, "one evening this good priest came in and said he had good news for me; he had had a long conversation with the Governor that day, and he thought that I would be permitted to return to my friends very shortly." The next day, in yet another interview, the governor told Meriwether he could return to the United States if he promised never to enter New Mexico again.

Vowing to follow the governor's orders, Meriwether and Alfred left Santa Fe with enough supplies to get them back to the United States. After spending an extremely cold winter on the Great Plains, during which the two men nearly starved and froze to death, the pair reached the Pawnee villages in February 1821. The following month, they arrived at their final destination, Council Bluffs.

Eventually Meriwether returned to the area around Louisville, Kentucky, where he married and sired thirteen children. He pursued various business interests until 1852, when he was appointed to fill a vacant seat in the U.S. Senate, created by the death of Henry Clay. In 1853 he broke his thirty-year-old promise never to return to New Mexico when President Franklin Pierce appointed him governor of that faraway land. Since 1820 the country had won its independence from Spain only to be occupied by the American army during the recent war with Mexico. Now an American territory, it was in need of a governor who understood the land and its people and who could peacefully settle the boundary dispute between the two nations.

The reception for Meriwether in New Mexico was grand. According to the *Santa Fe Gazette*,

> The procession ... moved on in calm and stately dignity to Santa Fe, through the principal entrance to the city until it reached the plaza in front of the Palace, or speaking more democratically, until the cortege was drawn up in front of the State, or Governor's house. Here the procession debarked, and thousands congregated to witness the formality of a public introduction of distinguished officers and the inauguration of the new Governor.

Meriwether served his territory well at an extremely difficult time in its existence. Animosities between the United States and Mexico remained, and the border was still in dispute. But Meriwether endured the storm and served as governor until 1857, when he resigned and returned to Kentucky. In 1914 another New Mexican territorial governor, L. Bradford Prince, wrote that Meriwether "made an intelligent, practical Governor" at a time when the territory was in turmoil.

Meriwether lived out his life at his home near Louisville, Kentucky. He died there in 1893, at the age of ninety-three.

1821

Fortune at the End of the Trail

William Becknell looked all around him, marveling at the vast landscape that differed so greatly from the farmland of his native Missouri. He thought he must be nearing his destination, but since he had never been to New Mexico before, he could not be sure. The thirty-three-year-old trader and his small party had left Missouri close to two months previously, intending to open a trading network with the Mexican citizens of Santa Fe.

As Becknell was about to move on, he spied a column of horsemen coming up the dusty trail from the southwest. His heart nearly stopped. They were soldiers, and judging from tales other American traders had told about being arrested and imprisoned by Spanish authorities in Santa Fe, he figured that he and his men were about to end up in the same predicament.

But Becknell noticed as the soldiers rode closer that they were not shooting or shouting or otherwise acting like arresting officers. Instead they were waving their arms and greeting the Americans like old friends. And he soon learned why. Through an interpreter, the Mexican commander informed him that Mexico had just won its independence from Spain. Not only would the new government tolerate free trade with Americans, it would actively seek relations. What a relief this news must have been to Becknell and his men as they rode the rest of the way to Santa Fe in the company of the soldiers.

In the capital city Becknell arranged an interview with the governor, Facundo Melgares, who confirmed the infant Mexican government's official position on American trade. Becknell later reported that the governor "expressed a desire that Americans would keep up an intercourse with that country and said that if any of them wished to emigrate, it would give him pleasure to afford them every facility."

The Mexican governor's promise of cooperation with American traders was just what Becknell wanted to hear. The news made his efforts of the past few months seem worthwhile. The previous June, based on rumors that Mexico might gain its independence—and based on the assumption that the new authorities would be more receptive to Americans than the old regime—Becknell had carefully planned this journey to Santa Fe. He had advertised in the *Missouri Intelligencer* for men to accompany him. The advertisement read:

> Every man will fit himself for the trip with a horse, a good rifle, and as much ammunition as the company may think necessary for a tour or 3 month trip, & sufficient cloathing [sic] to keep him warm and

comfortable. . . . It is requisite that every 8 men shall have a pack horse, an ax, and a tent to secure them from the inclemency of bad weather.

Becknell's party had left Arrow Rock, Missouri, on September 1, 1821, only a few days before Mexico would declare its independence. The outward journey carried the traders along what would eventually become the primary route of the Santa Fe Trail. From Missouri the men passed the sites of the future Kansas towns of Council Grove, Fort Larned, and Dodge City. They followed the Arkansas River upstream into today's Colorado and cut a thoroughfare southwestward through Raton Pass on the New Mexico border. Finally, they passed through the village of San Miguel and proceeded on to Santa Fe.

After Becknell had distributed his limited supply of trade goods among the rejoicing residents of Santa Fe, he returned to Missouri in a record forty-eight days. He immediately initiated plans for a second trip to New Mexico. The new expedition, which left Missouri in May 1822, was more extensive than Becknell's first effort. This time wagons instead of mules were used to carry loads many times larger than those of the previous year.

Because he knew he could not negotiate Raton Pass with wagons, Becknell charted a new course around today's Dodge City. He pointed his wagons southward and trekked across the dry region between the Arkansas and Cimarron Rivers. Later this route would be called the Cimarron Cutoff. Lack of water on the desert nearly killed Becknell, his men, and the mules that pulled the heavy wagons. Finally, however, they made it safely to New Mexico.

For his efforts in blazing the trail to New Mexico—a trail that hundreds of American traders hauling millions of pounds of freight would follow during the next six decades— William Becknell is called the "father" of the Santa Fe Trail. But he was not the first man to establish trade with the New Mexicans. As early as 1807, Jacques Clamorgan, a seventy-four-year-old fur entrepreneur from Saint Louis, had entered Santa Fe with four companions and four mules and had become the first American trader known to realize a profit in the Santa Fe trade. For the next ten years, several other Missourians made trips to New Mexico, but because Spanish authorities there were hostile toward most Americans and wary of their intense interest in the region, most of these traders were arrested and their goods confiscated.

However, with Mexican independence, things changed. Until the railroad reached New Mexico in the late 1870s, the Santa Fe Trail was the road of commerce, linking residents of the sleepy villages of New Mexico with the Missouri trading establishment.

1841

The Texan Santa Fe Expedition

A group of tired, frightened, and hungry Texans watched as New Mexico's infamous governor, Manuel Armijo, rode up to them on a large mule. The men were traveling the portion of the Santa Fe Trail that connected the New Mexican village of San Miguel with the capital city, some sixty miles to the west. They were members of the Texan Santa Fe Expedition, which had been organized in mid-1841 by Mirabeau B. Lamar, president of the Republic of Texas.

In June of that year, between three and four hundred men and boys, along with as many horses and a score of supply wagons, had left Austin, Texas, on the first leg of a journey whose mission, according to Lamar, was to open "a commercial intercourse with the people of Santa Fe." Additionally, wrote one of the chroniclers of the expedition, the leaders of the group would try to persuade New Mexican citizens to cast their political lots with the Republic. Then, "should the inhabitants really manifest a disposition to declare their full allegiance to Texas, the flag of the single-star Republic would have been raised on the Government House at Santa Fe."

However, the expedition had suffered severe logistical and supply problems in the vast West Texas plains. Its members had been captured and disarmed by elements of the Mexican army. Now, in the early fall of 1841, the men were marching toward their original destination of Santa Fe, but as prisoners of a hostile army. What was worse, they knew their fates lay in the hands of Armijo, a man with a vicious reputation.

One of the Americans in the party was George Wilkins Kendall, a thirty-two-year-old journalist from New Orleans who had learned his trade under the tutelage of Horace Greeley, founder of the *New York Tribune*. Kendall was a founder of the *New Orleans Picayune*, one of the most influential newspapers in the South. When he decided that he would like to make "a tour of some kind upon the great Western Prairies, induced by the hope of correcting a derangement of health," he signed on with the Texan Santa Fe Expedition and prepared for what he had hoped would be a pleasant journey. Kendall, with his own biases and interpretations, tells the story of this journey.

When the Mexican captors saw Armijo making his way toward their column, they ordered their prisoners to form a single line on the side of the road to show proper respect for the governor. As Armijo rode up on his mule, he politely greeted the captives and shook hands with each of them. He called them amigos, friends, and went out of his way to be cordial. However, when one of the Texans told Armijo that they were merchants, the governor grasped [him] by the collar of his dragoon jacket, dragged him up alongside his mule, and, pointing to the buttons, upon which were a single star and the word "Texas," he sternly said . . . "You need not think to deceive me: no merchant from the United States ever travels with a Texan military jacket."

Kendall had a valid passport, but when he showed it to Armijo, the governor replied that since the newspaperman had accompanied the others, who were clearly enemies of New Mexico, he would be detained with all the rest. Armijo then ordered one of his officers to march the captives back to San Miguel. When told that the men had already marched ten leagues and were too tired to walk farther, according to Kendall the angry Armijo retorted:

They are able to walk ten leagues more. . . . The Texans are active and untiring people—I know them. . . . If one of them pretends to be sick or tired on the road, shoot him down and bring me his ears! Go!

Back in San Miguel, affairs for the prisoners went from bad to worse. Kendall and his companions witnessed the execution of one of their compatriots, who was shot in the back by a Mexican soldier. After several weeks' confinement, they learned that they would all be marched to faraway Mexico City to stand trial for what Armijo perceived to be an invasion of Mexico. Finally, Kendall later wrote, on October 17, 1841:

after we had been paraded in the plaza of San Miguel, and the ceremony of counting up had been gone through, it was ascertained that the notorious Salezar—the greatest brute among Armijo's officers—was to have charge of us. This was considered unfortunate by all. . . . The beginning of a cold and disagreeable winter was at hand, as we set off on foot upon a journey of over two thousand miles—we were in the hands of a brute whose only delight was in cruelty and blood—should we be fortunate enough to withstand the fatigues attendant upon the journey, an uncertain fate awaited us at its termination.

After a weeks-long trek south to Mexico City, Kendall and his associates were imprisoned there. Most of them, including Kendall, were released in April 1842. Upon his arrival back home in New Orleans, he began to write an exhaustive history of his experiences with the Texan Santa Fe Expedition. In 1844, his two-volume book was published in New York under the hefty title *Narrative of the Texan Santa Fe Expedition: Comprising a Description of a Tour Through Texas.*

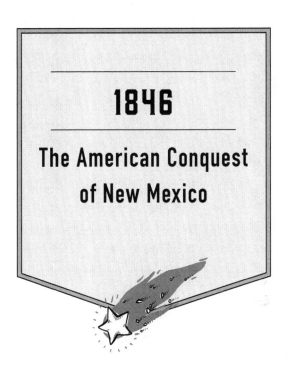

1846

The American Conquest of New Mexico

On the evening of August 14, 1846, Colonel Stephen Watts Kearny and an army of nearly seventeen hundred regular American soldiers and Missouri volunteers approached the small village of Las Vegas, nestled beside the Santa Fe Trail in today's San Miguel County, New Mexico. Kearny and his men were about to complete the first of two objectives assigned to them the previous June after the United States declared war on Mexico. Kearny's orders, issued at his headquarters at Fort Leavenworth, Missouri, were to conquer New Mexico and California for the United States.

Kearny and his men had wasted no time getting started on their mission. Leaving Fort Leavenworth in late June, the "Army of the West," as the column was called, headed west along the Santa Fe Trail, with additional instructions to "establish temporary civil governments" in New Mexico and California and to "act in such a manner as best to conciliate the inhabitants, and render them friendly to the United States."

The logistics of Kearny's command were mind-boggling. With him, in addition to the 1,700 troops, were 3,658 mules, 14,904 cattle, 459 horses, and 1,556 wagons. His artillery command consisted of twelve cannons and four howitzers. The sheer magnitude of moving an entourage of such proportions across hundreds of miles of dry, provisionless prairie was staggering. But Kearny was a seasoned veteran of the First Dragoons, and he took the matter in stride as his several-mile-long column crossed the dusty southern Great Plains.

As the Army of the West approached the outskirts of Las Vegas, the colonel received two messages. One, from Washington, D.C., advised him that he had been promoted to brigadier general. The other was an intelligence report stating that about six hundred Mexican soldiers, fully prepared for battle, had assembled in a pass two miles away. Kearny ordered his command to pitch camp for the night and prepare for the coming day's battle.

At 8:00 a.m. on the following day, August 15, Kearny and a few staff officers rode into the plaza at Las Vegas. From the rooftop of a nearby building, Kearny proclaimed the American occupation of New Mexico. He made a moving speech to his intent listeners, pleading with them not to resist his army and promising them they would be treated fairly. He declared:

> I have come amongst you by the orders of my government, to take possession of your country, and

extend over it the laws of the United States. We consider it, and have done so for some time, a part of the territory of the United States. We come amongst you as friends—not as enemies; as protectors—not as conquerors. We come among you for your benefit—not for your injury.

Henceforth, I absolve you from all allegiance to the Mexican government, and from all obedience to General Armijo [the Mexican governor]. . . . I shall not expect you to take up arms and follow me, to fight your own people who may oppose me; but I tell you now, that those who remain peaceably at home, attending to their crops and their herds, shall be protected by me in their property, their persons, and their religion. . . . But listen! he who promises to be quiet, and is found in arms against me, I will hang.

After administering an oath of allegiance to the United States to several village officials, Kearny ordered his army toward Santa Fe and a rendezvous with the six-hundred-man Mexican army that supposedly awaited him. As it turned out, the report was false, and Kearny encountered no hostile soldiers. Reaching San Miguel the next day, he read its citizens a speech similar to the one he had made at Las Vegas. He also received another message that a large Mexican force, under the command of Governor Armijo, was poised to defend Apache Canyon, on the outskirts of Santa Fe.

However, unbeknown to his soldiers, Kearny had sent James Magoffin, a Santa Fe trader, and Captain Philip Saint George Cooke to Santa Fe to secretly negotiate the surrender of the town. Earlier in the year Magoffin had met with President James K. Polk in Washington and had been commissioned as government agent for the purpose of effecting a bloodless conquest of New Mexico.

Magoffin had met secretly with Governor Armijo and had received his promise not to defend Santa Fe. When the Army of the West approached Apache Canyon on August 18, Kearny found that Armijo had lived up to his vow and called off the defense of the canyon. The soldiers in Kearny's command were jubilant. Unaware of the secret negotiations in Santa Fe, they gloried in their military prowess, confident that the Mexican army had fled out of fear.

Kearny's troops were now only twenty-nine miles from Santa Fe. One of his staff officers, Lieutenant W. H. Emory, later reported that "not a hostile rifle or arrow was now between the army and Santa Fe, the capital of New Mexico, and the general determined to make the march in one day, and raise the United States flag over the palace before sundown."

Around noon, two Mexicans approached Kearny, one of them the acting secretary of state. He carried a letter from the lieutenant governor assuring Kearny that he would encounter no resistance and extending to him what hospitality the town had to offer. The advance elements of the army reached Santa Fe at around 3:00 p.m., and the rear guard pulled into town three hours later. The lieutenant governor invited Kearny's staff to the governor's palace for refreshments, and in Emory's words, "as the sun was sitting [sic], the United States flag was hoisted over the palace, and a salute of thirteen guns fired from the artillery planted on the eminence overlooking the town."

The American occupation of New Mexico was now complete. On August 22, Kearny issued a proclamation to the people of Santa Fe spelling out exactly what was expected of them, at the same time declaring that he intended "to hold the department [New Mexico], with its original boundaries ... as part of the United States, and under the name of the Territory of New Mexico."

Kearny was pleased with his bloodless conquest. In a letter to General Jonathan E. Wool, the army commander at Chihuahua, he proudly declared: "Every thing here is quiet and peaceable. The people now understand the advantages they are to derive from a change of government, and are much gratified with it."

On September 22, Kearny appointed Charles Bent, a well-known and respected American trader and resident of the nearby town of Taos, as governor of New Mexico Territory. His mission in New Mexico now completed, the general continued on to California. But in his joy over the successful occupation of New Mexico, he was oblivious to an undercurrent of dissatisfaction among some of the territory's residents. In a few months the pot of discontent would boil over, and it would be the new governor, Charles Bent, who would suffer the consequences.

1847

The Murder of Charles Bent

harles Bent, governor of the new American territory of New Mexico, was tired as he approached his home in the village of Taos, about sixty-two miles north of Santa Fe. He had left Santa Fe the previous day, January 17, 1847, and his plan was to take a few days off work to be with his wife, Maria, and the couple's several children. Affairs in the capital city had been hectic for the past few weeks, and Bent was beginning to feel the tremendous pressure of supervising the complex transition from Mexican government to American.

It was late in the evening when Bent reached his home, a modest adobe house one block north of the town plaza. Bent had been one of the village's most prominent citizens since his arrival in the mid-1830s. He was a trader known for his fairness and honesty. With his brother William and a friend, Ceran Saint Vrain, he had built Bent's Fort in the early 1830s on the Arkansas River near today's town of La Junta, Colorado. Bent's Fort had rapidly become the hub of a vast fur and buffalo-robe trading empire that included all or parts of today's states of Wyoming, Utah, Colorado, New Mexico, Arizona, Texas, Oklahoma, Kansas, and Nebraska. Over the years Bent had made many friends in his adopted home. His wife, the former Maria Ignacia Jaramillo, had been a well-to-do widow when Bent married her, and her high standing in the community had helped to establish him as a man of great importance and influence in the region.

After chatting with Maria and the children for a while, Bent and his family prepared for bed. Sometime during the early morning hours of January 19, the entire household was awakened by what sounded like shouting in the street out front. Climbing out of bed, still half asleep, Bent walked down the hall and opened the front door, only to be confronted by dozens of Mexicans and Taos. Although the governor had heard rumors of unrest in the area for some time—and in fact had assisted in defusing a potentially dangerous situation in December—he had never seriously considered that his friends and neighbors would resort to violence. As he studied the crowd on his doorstep, he quickly realized that he was wrong.

Bent tried to calm the unruly crowd, but to no avail. Within seconds he was wounded several times, and when he fell to the ground, he was scalped alive. In the meantime, Mrs. Bent, along with her sister, Mrs. Kit Carson, and the children, managed to cut a hole through one of the thick adobe walls of the house using only a poker and a large spoon. Escaping to the courtyard, they found temporary respite from the violence. The dying governor followed them outside.

The attackers soon surrounded the survivors in the courtyard, where Bent died. The women and children were spared, and according to Bent's daughter, Teresina, who testified against the murderers later in the spring, they were left alone with their "great sorrow." Bent's attackers told his Mexican neighbors to offer no assistance to the distraught women and children. Teresina's testimony continued:

> We were without food and had no covering but our night-clothing, all that day and the next night. The body of our father remained on the floor in a pool of blood. We were naturally frightened, as we did not know how soon the miscreants might return to do us violence. At about three o'clock the next morning, some of our Mexican friends stole up to the house and gave us food and clothing. That day, also, they took my father to bury him.

The revolutionaries were not content with only the American governor's blood. Before the day was out, they killed and mutilated five more Americans and Mexicans who sympathized with the Americans. According to official records the other victims were Stephen Lee, sheriff; James W. Leal, the circuit attorney; Cornelio Vigil, a prefect; Narciso Beaubien, the son of the circuit judge; and Pablo Jaramillo, Mrs. Bent's brother.

Although more violence was yet to come, the rampage of the revolutionaries at Taos on January 19 constituted the major effort on their part to destroy once and for all anyone and anything related to the American presence in New Mexico.

Their plan did not work. Immediately after the Taos incident, the U.S. Army was placed on full alert. The commanding officer, Colonel Sterling Price, assembled as many soldiers as he could and marched north from Santa Fe toward Taos Pueblo on January 23. After a couple of skirmishes with rebels along the way, he and his command reached the pueblo in early February. They found it to be "a place of great strength, being surrounded by adobe walls and strong pickets," Price later said. However, after two days of heavy fighting, during which 150 rebels were killed and the church in which they sought refuge destroyed, the Native and Mexican revolutionaries sued for peace. Two ringleaders were arrested and bound over for trial, but an American soldier killed one of them while the man was in jail.

The other perpetrator, along with several other Taos and Mexicans, was tried in Taos in April. They were convicted of murder or treason and hanged. Less than a year later, the Mexican–American War ended, and New Mexico officially became part of the United States. The bloodshed in Taos and the surrounding countryside in early 1847 turned out to be for naught.

1847

Battle at Turley's Mill

Simeon Turley was a happy man. With his Mexican wife, Maria, the Kentucky-born, Missouri-bred trader lived in his combination flour mill and whiskey distillery at a place called Arroyo Hondo, just a few miles north of Taos. He had arrived in New Mexico some twenty years earlier, and now, midway through January 1847, he was enjoying the fruits of his success.

The strong whiskey that Turley distilled later became known as "Taos Lightning," and fur trappers, traders, and Native Americans came from miles around to bargain for the almost-pure alcohol. His trading post and flour mill were equally successful, and all in all, Turley considered that life had treated him well indeed.

On January 19, Turley was hosting a kind of reunion—in fact, a sort of indoor, old-time rendezvous—of several of his former mountain-man friends. Eight trappers had come out of the wilderness, most of them from the settlement that later became Pueblo, Colorado, and dropped down through the forested southern Rocky Mountains to Turley's Mill. Everyone intended to have a good time reminiscing about the good old days, eating Maria's fine cooking, and drinking plenty of Turley's stout whiskey. Although Turley had been warned that an insurrection among the Mexicans and their Taos allies was imminent, he had paid little heed to the rumors. After all, he was married to a Mexican woman and was well liked and respected in the neighborhood. His sense of security was shattered when, on the morning of January 19, a lone rider rode up to his gate and exclaimed that Governor Charles Bent and several others had just been killed by revolutionaries in Taos.

Turley assembled his guests and apprised them of the situation. Fortunately all of the mountain men were well armed, and it did not take long for the group to organize itself into a small army. Turley closed the gates, barricaded the windows, and gathered extra rifles together. Soon a large party of Mexicans and Native Americans approached the mill and demanded the surrender of Turley's friends, promising that no harm would come to Turley. George Ruxton, an English writer most remembered for his firsthand accounts of the mountain men and their way of life, wrote in 1847 that, "to this summons Turley answered that he would never surrender his house nor his men, and that, if they wanted it or them, 'they must take them.'"

The situation was at an impasse. The odds were overwhelming. Five hundred or more rebels poised themselves outside the walls of Turley's Mill, ready to attack the nine defenders of the distillery. Turley would not budge. He had meant what he said, and when it became apparent to the assailants that there would be no surrender, they attacked.

The fighting continued all day, and as night approached, the Mexicans and Native Americans pulled back and planned how they might finish off Turley and his friends the next morning. All night the vigilant inhabitants of the mill stood watch, "running balls, cutting patches, and completing the defences [sic] of the building," according to Ruxton.

The vicious fighting resumed the following morning. By then the enemy force had grown, and several attackers had infiltrated part of the courtyard. As the fighting continued into the late morning, two of Turley's friends were killed. Ammunition supplies within the mill started running low. The rebels set fire to several outbuildings, and it became increasingly apparent to Turley's men that further defense was useless in the face of such overwhelming numbers.

Turley held a powwow with the survivors, and they decided that each man should attempt to escape on his own. At dusk on the second night of the siege, the defenders of Turley's Mill made a break, scattering in all directions as soon as they cleared the compound's walls. In the end only three men escaped alive, including Turley. But the ordeal was not over for the determined trader and his two comrades. When Turley had traveled far enough from the mill to feel safe, he met a Mexican acquaintance and pleaded with the man to help him escape the angry rebels still prowling the countryside. He even gave the man his cherished watch as an incentive. The man promised to return shortly with help, but when he came back, he brought several Mexican rebels with him. One of them calmly pulled a pistol and shot Simeon Turley dead.

The two men who had fled the mill with Turley, Thomas Tobin and John Albert, made good their escape. Tobin fled to Santa Fe, and Albert finally drifted into Pueblo, Colorado, a tired and ragged remnant of a man. When the mountain-man fraternity there heard what had happened at Taos and Turley's Mill, they mounted an expedition and headed south. Some of them participated in the final destruction of the revolutionaries at Taos Pueblo in February 1847, and a few witnessed the executions of the rebels in Taos the following April.

Turley's wife, Maria, escaped harm. When order was restored in the Taos Valley, she and several of Turley's brothers and sisters inherited his estate—or at least what was left of it after the attack and subsequent destruction of much of his property. Maria was still living there in 1883.

Albert eventually gave up the mountain life and settled in Walsenburg, Colorado, where he died in 1899. Tobin became a guide in California and died in 1904. He was buried at Fort Garland, Colorado.

1862

The Gettysburg
of the West

He was still a young man in 1862, but Alfred B. Peticolas had already worked his way up to sergeant in the Confederate Fourth Texas Mounted Volunteers. Stationed in remote New Mexico, he often wondered how the same Civil War that Union officials were boasting would be over within a few months had only recently had any impact out here. Peticolas and his companions—men of the Fourth, Fifth, and Seventh Texas Volunteers—had so far seen only limited action, and fortunately for them, most of the skirmishes in which they had participated had been decided in their favor.

In December 1861, General Henry Hopkins Sibley had arrived in El Paso, Texas, and assumed command of all Confederate troops in the West. Then, in February 1862, he had attacked Union-occupied Fort Craig in New Mexico and defeated Colonel Edward R. S. Canby at the Battle of Valverde. Quickly following up on his victory, Sibley had marched on Albuquerque and Santa Fe and had easily taken both towns. Now the only force of any consequence standing between his army and Denver was a small garrison of U.S. soldiers at Fort Union, on the Santa Fe Trail east of the capital. Sibley set up his command post in Albuquerque, and from there he sent units of the Texas Volunteers to take Fort Union.

Though the Confederates had enjoyed earlier victories in New Mexico, today would be different. It was March 28, 1862, and the one thousand officers and men of the Texas Mounted Riflemen were unaware that Jefferson Davis's Confederate States of America was about to lose its foothold in New Mexico and the Southwest once and for all.

Two days previously, men of the Fifth Texas had fought with Major John Chivington's First Colorado Volunteers at Apache Canyon, a narrow defile through which the Santa Fe Trail passed. After fighting practically all day, Chivington's men finally seized the advantage and routed the Confederates. However, since nightfall was rapidly approaching, Chivington failed to pursue the retreating Texans, who fell back to fight another day.

In the meantime, Major L. Pyron, the Confederate commander at Apache Canyon, sent an urgent request for help to Lieutenant Colonel W. F. Scurry, who was encamped at nearby Galisteo. Scurry responded the following day with more men and eighty supply wagons and parked the vehicles at Johnson's Ranch, not far from Apache Canyon. When Union forces failed to attack all that day, Scurry took the offensive on the morning of March 28. His command now consisted of about seven hundred soldiers from the Fourth,

Fifth, and Seventh Texas Volunteers, plus three cannons. Left behind to guard the supply wagons were about two hundred Texans.

Scurry ran into Union positions commanded by Colonel John P. Slough near Pigeon's Ranch. Fierce fighting ensued. Peticolas was there, and afterward he wrote his impressions of the action.

> We charged up a hill towards an enemy who were hidden and invisible and who waited patiently for us to approach to shoot us down. Up we went, taking advantage of every bush and tree to shelter us. We saw no foe till in twenty yards of them, and then they rose from behind their breast works of rocks and poured into us a deadly volley.

After battling for five hours, both sides counted their casualties. Thirty-six Texans had been killed and sixty wounded. Scurry himself had been injured, and he revealed in his official report of March 30 that

> Major Pyron had his horse shot under him, and my own cheek was twice bruised by a Minie ball, each time drawing blood, and my clothes torn in two places. I mention this simply to show how hot was the fire of the enemy when all of the field officers upon the ground were either killed or touched. . . . I do not know if I write intelligently. I have not slept for three nights, and can scarcely hold my eyes open.

Twenty-nine of Slough's Union troops were killed, forty-two wounded, and fifteen taken prisoner. Actually, the battle was a near draw, but then Scurry received word that his wagon encampment had been attacked and destroyed. With that devastating news, the wounded Confederate leader requested a cease-fire.

Later, the Texans learned how their supply wagons had been compromised and lost. Major Chivington and his First Colorado Volunteers had crossed the mountains south of the main road that skirted Pigeon's Ranch and arrived unnoticed at the wagon park. The few surprised Texans who guarded the vehicles were no match for Chivington's riflemen. All eighty wagons—containing food, ammunition, and other critical supplies—were burned. The horses and mules that pulled them were killed, and seventeen Texans were captured.

Meanwhile, back at Pigeon's Ranch, the cease-fire went into effect, and as Union troops watched from nearby Kozlowski's Ranch, the men of the Texas Volunteer units slowly retreated. What had started as a grand invasion of New Mexico had now suddenly become an embarrassing rout. On March 31, a frantic General Sibley reported to Adjutant General Samuel Cooper in Richmond, Virginia, that

> [p]ending the battle the enemy detached a portion of his forces to attack and destroy our supply train, which he succeeded in doing, thus crippling Colonel Scurry to such a degree that he was two days without provisions or blankets. . . . In consequence of the loss of his train Colonel Scurry has fallen back upon Santa Fe. . . . I must have re-enforcements. . . . Send me re-enforcements.

With the two, day-long engagements at Apache Canyon and Pigeon's Ranch—collectively known as the Battle of Glorieta Pass and sometimes referred to by historians as "the Gettysburg of the West"—Confederate dreams of dominating

New Mexico Territory faded rapidly. General Sibley and the remainder of his army eventually retreated all the way to El Paso, and the Union controlled the territory for the remainder of the war.

1866

An Apache Kidnapping

Andres Martinez was probably less than ten years old in October 1866, when he and his even younger nephew, Pedro, left the family ranch near Las Vegas, New Mexico, to take his father's cattle to pasture. The rangeland the cattle grazed was only a few miles from home, and Andres's father, Juan, promised to bring the boys lunch at noon. After spending the morning talking, playing, and watching the cattle, Andres and Pedro heard men talking in the distance. Assuming the approaching voices were those of his father and brothers, Andres, joined by Pedro, ran across the meadows toward the sounds.

As the boys cleared a slight knoll, they spied a small band of Apache warriors approaching. Dropping to the ground before the Apache could see them, the two lads noticed that the Apache were observing an old Mexican man, who, along with two burros loaded with flour, was traveling toward the small village of San Geronimo. The Apache passed the boys, and when Andres and Pedro thought it was safe to move, they ran for the path that led back to their family's ranch. They had only traveled a few yards when they were confronted by two mounted Apache, who for some reason had separated from their tribesmen. The warriors took the two boys prisoner and rejoined their companions, who, in the meantime, had captured the Mexican and stripped him of his clothing. Within minutes they had killed the old man.

Several days after the boys' seizure, the Apache also killed little Pedro, who was unable to keep up their rapid pace. When he attempted to help his nephew, Andres was struck in the forehead with a spear, causing a scar that was plainly visible for the rest of his life. Leaving Pedro's body where it had fallen, the Apache and Andres moved westward, crossed the Pecos River, and finally reached the main Native American camp a few days later.

Andres's reception at the Apache camp was less than he had hoped for but about what he had expected. Most of the Apache made fun of him, struck him as he passed by, and generally made his life miserable for the next few weeks. Although it was difficult to accept, Andres decided that he was never going to be rescued and that his new life among the Apache would never improve. One day, about two months after his capture and while he was tending to his chores, Andres was told that a band of Kiowa braves was about to enter camp. The Kiowas had accidentally run into a small party of Apache, and since neither group was in a position strong enough to attack, the leaders of the two groups had arranged a temporary peace while both tribes were in the neighborhood. The Kiowas pitched camp beside a stream in a small meadow near the Apache encampment.

Before the Kiowas moved on, they bought Andres from the Apache. The youth had caught the eye of Chief Heap O' Bears, who wanted to give him to his daughter to raise in place of her recently deceased son. At last Andres had escaped his Apache tormentors. Heap O' Bears gave the boy a new name, "Andele." After traveling many miles through New Mexico, the Kiowa band, with Andele riding proudly beside his adopted grandfather, turned northeastward and started its long trip home to the Washita River region in today's state of Oklahoma.

Andele lived among the Kiowa for nearly twenty years. During his stay he grew to manhood, became a warrior, and married a Kiowa woman, who within a few months left him for another man. He married again and lived with this wife until her death. He had forgotten most of his former life.

When Andele heard a U.S. Indian agent explaining to the Kiowa the plans the government had for them, and how they could become farmers with property and income of their own, he decided to give it a try. The agent found him a job in a blacksmith shop. Andele told the blacksmith that he had been kidnapped by the Apache years ago, and after considerable thought, he remembered his name was Martinez. He persuaded the local government physician to write to his family. On January 6, 1883, Dr. Hugh Tobin wrote from the Kiowa and Comanche agency at Anadarko, Indigenous Territory, to the man in Las Vegas whom Andele believed to be his brother. The letter read:

Dear Sir: Did you have a little brother stolen by the Indians many years ago, by name Andres? The

Indians call him Andele. If so, write me at once. He is here, and we think can be identified fully.

The letter came back unclaimed, as did several others over the next two years. Finally one of the letters did get through to Andele's brother while he was visiting his mother in Las Vegas. Within days the brother was on his way to Indigenous Territory to pick up the long-lost Andres.

Andres stayed with his mother and the remainder of his family until 1889, during which time he relearned Spanish and recovered most of his people's customs and ways. His Kiowa wife, in the meantime, had died. Eventually he returned to his Kiowa family in Oklahoma and was baptized in the Methodist Church. Several months later he took a position as interpreter and industrial teacher at the Methvin Institute near Anadarko, where he instructed his Native American friends. In 1893 Andres married Emma McWhorter, the daughter of a Methodist minister.

1880

Showdown in Las Vegas

I t was January 1880, and the weather had turned cold in the vicinity of Las Vegas, New Mexico. Late in the month, four cowboys—Tom Henry, John Dorsey, James West, and William Randall—rode into the small village, intent on warming themselves with some good whiskey. While they were there, they decided they might as well gamble a little and treat themselves to some female companionship. By the time long shadows stretched across the dry prairie that surrounded Las Vegas, the four visitors were drunk and making nuisances of themselves.

Local law officials attempted to reason with the four men, politely asking them to turn in their weapons until they were ready to leave town. The cowboys flatly refused to part with their revolvers. For a while the sheriff did not force the issue, hoping the situation would resolve itself. But finally, after several days of hard drinking had turned the four cowboys into real troublemakers, Sheriff Joe Carson made his move.

On the evening of January 22, Carson confronted the four men at the Close and Patterson dance hall in East Las Vegas. This newer—and wilder—part of town had sprung up with the arrival of the railroad the previous year. The men were still drunk, and this time Carson insisted that they disarm while in town. They refused again, cursing and laughing derisively. As Carson backed away from the foursome, one of them pulled a pistol and fired. Carson drew one of his two pistols and shot twice. By this time all the drunken cowboys were shooting, and Carson fell to the floor. In the meantime, Carson's deputy, David Mather, opened fire on the rowdies. When the shooting stopped, Carson and Randall lay dead, and West was writhing with the pain of a gunshot wound to his stomach. Observers reported that nearly forty rounds had been fired in less than one minute.

Dorsey, unscathed, and Henry, limping because of a gunshot wound in the leg, took off for the Lewelling and Olds Corral. They stole two horses and quickly left town. West was carted off to jail. Mather covered Carson's body and sent a bystander up the street to fetch the undertaker.

Two days later the local newspaper, the *Optic*, shed more light on the incident.

Today we visited Mrs. Carson, who is heart-broken and disconsolate over the brutal murder of her husband. She has his garments, which are perforated with bullet holes, carefully folded away in her trunk. There are eight bullet holes in his coat, and one in his boot, showing that he was shot nine times. . . . On the night he met his death, Joe had two revolvers on his person—one in a scabbard around his body and one in his hip pocket. The chambers in the latter one were empty and, as traces of blood are visible, it is thought that poor Joe managed to get it out of his pocket and fire two shots at his assailants.

A couple of weeks after the shootout, the two men who had escaped, Henry and Dorsey, were sighted several miles away in Mora County. A posse rode off toward the tiny village of Mora, nestled in the mountains some thirty miles to the north.

Surprisingly the two fugitives surrendered peacefully to the posse. On February 6, residents of Las Vegas gathered around the jail as the murderers were led to their awaiting cells. The mob questioned the posse members about whether the captives had shown any remorse, but all they could learn was that the prisoners blamed the entire unfortunate affair on "whiskey."

Henry and Dorsey did not have long to think about their fates. On their second night in the county jail, they and West were yanked out of their cells by a crowd of angry citizens and marched to the windmill that stood in the middle of the plaza in Las Vegas. Nooses were placed around the three men's necks, and they were asked if they had any last words. Someone gave the signal and tightened the ropes. The first of the killers, West, dropped from the platform of the windmill and, as the crowd watched, his body swung back and forth in the slight winter's breeze.

But Sheriff Carson's widow thought hanging was too good for these outlaws. She stepped from the crowd and started firing a rifle into the bodies of her husband's killers.

The rest of the spectators joined in and, when the shooting stopped, all three desperadoes were dead, their limp bodies riddled with bullets.

A coroner's jury was convened to investigate the deaths. Its verdict was clear and straightforward. It found no wrongdoing on the part of Mrs. Carson or any other citizen. It did find that Henry and Dorsey "came to death by several shots in their heads," and that West displayed "signs of being hanged by the neck by some person or persons unknown." The verdict ended with the statement, "We also found that the doors of the jail were broken open and from investigation we learn that the above men [the killers] were taken out of their cells by a mob, unknown to this jury."

Miguel A. Otero, New Mexico's territorial governor from 1897 to 1906, once wrote:

> For more than a year after the entry of the railroad, it can be stated without fear of contradiction that Las Vegas was the "hottest" town in the country. Such a statement would be substantiated by the record, for one month, which ... old files ... establish. They show that twenty-nine men were killed in and around Las Vegas, either murdered outright or shot in self-defense or hung by the well-regulated Vigilance Committee. Such a record, I am certain, would be hard to parallel in the history of any of the wild towns of the West.

1880

Sergeant Jordan's
Medal of Honor

C hief Victorio was a persistent man. For a month in 1877, he
and his Apache followers refused to settle on the desolate
San Carlos Reservation as the U.S. government had ordered
them to do. Finally, he and his people surrendered to the
army and were sent to Ojo Caliente, their tribal homeland,
until officials could decide their fate. When word came from
the Indian Bureau that Victorio and his band must return to
San Carlos, the chief bolted and headed for the mountains.
Hopes for a peaceful solution to the problem ended in September 1879, when he and sixty warriors killed eight black
troopers of the Ninth Cavalry near Ojo Caliente.

Sergeant George Jordan of Troop K, Ninth Cavalry,
knew all about Victorio. Only recently he had been told that
about one hundred Apache under Victorio's command were

marching toward the town of Tularosa, New Mexico, and he had orders to protect its citizens. As he and the twenty-five troopers in his command hastened to the town's defense on May 14, 1880, he thought of all the trouble the Apache chief had caused the army. He wondered what it would be like to come face-to-face with this legendary man, whom he knew was a worthy successor to the famous chiefs Mangas Coloradas and Cochise. Jordan figured that he would find out before long, as each minute brought him closer to his Apache foe.

Jordan had been born in Williamson County, Tennessee, in 1848. When the Civil War ended, he traveled to nearby Nashville and enlisted in the army. He eventually became a member of the Ninth Cavalry, an all-black regiment commanded by white officers. It, and the all-black Tenth Cavalry, and Twenty-Fourth and Twenty-Fifth infantry regiments, were sent West, and over the next few years, they fought in many major Native engagements. They were one of the most effective weapons in the army's arsenal during the Southwestern Indian wars of the 1870s and 1880s. The black soldiers quickly earned the respect of their Native American foes, who called them "Buffalo Soldiers."

Colonel Benjamin Henry Grierson, the white commander of the Tenth Cavalry, summed up the attitude that most career army officers had toward the Buffalo Soldiers. He once remarked that

> the officers and enlisted men have cheerfully endured
> many hardships and privations, and in the midst of
> great dangers steadfastly maintained a most gallant
> and zealous devotion to duty ... and they may well
> be proud of the record made, and rest assured that

the hard work undergone in the accomplishment of such ... valuable service to their country cannot fail, sooner or later, to meet with due recognition and reward.

Although Jordan was only five feet, four and one-half inches tall, he was a giant among his troopers. A natural-born leader, he always seemed to be at the right place at the right time, a trait appreciated by the younger enlisted men in his command. He was only thirty-two years old himself, but to the others in the troop, he was already an old veteran, unscathed by many an encounter with hostile Natives Americans.

As Jordan and his men approached Tularosa, they saw more than a hundred Apache riding toward them. It was obvious that the troopers were vastly outnumbered. Nonetheless Jordan urged his men onward. They reached the town just before the Apache, and soon a fierce battle ensued. For several minutes Victorio and his warriors tried to dislodge Jordan and his twenty-five troopers from their defensive positions. All efforts failed.

The Apache fired into a nearby herd of cattle, hoping to stampede the beasts through town and force Jordan's men to withdraw. That ploy failed, also. Finally, after suffering several casualties themselves, the Apache retreated and left the village of Tularosa in peace.

For his bravery under fire and his success in defeating Victorio's superior forces that day at Tularosa, Sergeant George Jordan was presented the Medal of Honor, the highest award obtainable by an American soldier.

The Buffalo Soldiers went on to fight in the Spanish-American War, where they helped other elements of the U.S. Army overrun Spanish defenses in Cuba. They served in the

Philippines, and in 1916 they rode with one of their old officers, General John J. "Black Jack" Pershing (the name Black Jack came from Pershing's former duty with the all-black Tenth Cavalry) into Mexico in pursuit of Pancho Villa, after the bandit had raided Columbus, New Mexico. Later, during the Korean War, the Buffalo Soldiers were integrated into the rest of the army.

Sergeant Jordan was commended again for valor during a battle with the Apache at Carrizo Canyon, New Mexico, in 1881. He retired from the army years later. The old warrior died on October 24, 1904.

1881

The Death of Billy the Kid

Billy the Kid felt exhausted as he bedded down in Pete Maxwell's house in Fort Sumner, New Mexico. It was mid-July 1881, and the slightly built, bucktoothed boy, who sometimes went by the name Henry Antrim and other times called himself Henry McCarty, was on the run again. This time he was trying to evade Sheriff Pat Garrett, who was on his trail for escaping from a makeshift jail in the Lincoln County Courthouse on April 28. During the breakout, the Kid had killed two men, deputies Robert Olinger and James W. Bell.

The Kid had already been found guilty of murder in Mesilla, New Mexico, on April 13. There, Judge Warren H. Bristol of the Third Judicial District had ordered him to be held in Lincoln until May 13, 1881, when he was to be "hanged by the neck until his body be dead." He had spent only a week in the Lincoln jail before escaping.

On the day of the escape, Sheriff Garrett had been out of town collecting taxes. He had left Olinger and Bell in charge of the Kid and several other prisoners. Around noon Olinger assembled the prisoners to take them across the street to the Wortley Hotel for lunch. The Kid asked permission to go to the privy behind the courthouse. While Olinger escorted the other prisoners to lunch, Billy reportedly recovered a pistol that someone had left for him in the outhouse and killed Bell.

The Kid watched out the second-floor window of the courthouse, armed with Olinger's own double-barreled shotgun, as the deputy scampered back across the street at the sound of gunfire. The courthouse custodian, Godfrey Gauss, yelled at Olinger that the Kid had just killed Bell. Just then Olinger saw Billy in the upstairs window aiming the shotgun at him. "Yes, and he's killed me too," were reportedly Olinger's last words before Billy dropped him in a pool of blood.

About an hour after the killings, Billy the Kid mounted up and left Lincoln for the last time. He met with no resistance from any of the townspeople, causing Sheriff Garrett to remark later that

> the inhabitants of the whole town of Lincoln appeared to be terror-stricken. The Kid, it is my firm belief, could have ridden up and down the plaza until dark without a shot having been fired at him, nor an attempt made to arrest him. A little sympathy might have actuated some of them, but most of the people were, doubtless, paralyzed with fear when it was

whispered that the dreaded desperado, the Kid, was at liberty and had slain his guards.

One of Billy's legs was still in shackles when he left Lincoln on a stolen horse. He stopped at a friend's ranch nearby and removed the cuff. Then he made a fateful decision. Instead of heading south into Mexico, where he could escape the posse that he knew would soon follow him, he chose to ride to Fort Sumner, a town he knew well. The Kid's poor judgment and perhaps a lack of appreciation for Sheriff Garrett's tenacity proved to be his undoing.

After several weeks of searching for the Kid, Garrett learned that he was in Fort Sumner. Finding it hard to believe that Billy would return to a town in which he was so well-known, Garrett decided to check out the information anyway. With two deputies he rode to Fort Sumner, arriving on the night of July 14, 1881. When the three lawmen pulled up in front of Pete Maxwell's house, Garrett told his men to wait outside while he interviewed Maxwell. Garrett disappeared into the house.

Soon afterward the Kid stepped onto the porch on his way to the meat house to retrieve a beefsteak for supper. Since neither of Garrett's deputies had ever seen either the Kid or Maxwell, they had no reason to suspect this man who strolled across the porch in his stocking feet. One of the deputies, John W. Poe, assumed that "the man approaching was either Maxwell or some guest who might have been staying there." He went on to describe what happened next:

> He came on until he was almost within an arm's length of where I sat, before he saw me, as I was partially concealed from his view by the post of the gate. Upon his seeing me, he covered me with his

six-shooter as quick as lightning, sprang onto the porch, calling out in Spanish, "¿Quién es?" (Who is it?)—at the same time backing away from me toward the door through which Garrett only a few seconds before had passed, repeating his query, "Who is it?" in Spanish several times.

The Kid bolted back inside. Garrett, catching the Kid's silhouette in the moonlight, drew his revolver and shot twice. Billy the Kid fell dead to the floor.

The following day Garrett wrote to the governor of New Mexico Territory, Lionel A. Sheldon, to tell him that Billy had died from a gunshot wound that "struck him in the left breast and pierced his heart." A coroner's jury cleared Garrett of any wrongdoing and further stated that "we are united in opinion that the gratitude of all the community is due to said Garrett for his action, and that he deserves to be compensated."

The name of no other outlaw in American history may be as widely recognized as that of Billy the Kid. Yet some of his past is still shrouded in mystery. The best indications are that he was born in New York City in 1859, the son of Patrick and Catherine Devine McCarty. After Patrick died around 1864, Catherine and her children moved to Wichita, Kansas, and in 1873 to Santa Fe, New Mexico, where she married William H. Antrim. It was in New Mexico that the Kid picked up his most common alias, William Bonney.

So much has been written over the past century and a half about Billy the Kid that it is possible for one to draw just about any conclusion about the youth's short life. Garrett acknowledged that Billy "was open-handed, generous-hearted, frank, and manly." But other more recent writers have not been so kind. One historian, Jeff Dykes, once called the Kid "that mythical hero, the Robin Hood of the Southwest, who was once just a buck-toothed, thieving, murderous, little cowboy-gone-bad."

Whether Billy was a "little cowboy-gone-bad" or whether he was rotten from the start is a question that will be debated for as long as the olden days of the American West are discussed and studied. One thing is certain, however. Garrett shot and killed an American legend at Pete Maxwell's house on the night of July 14, 1881.

1884

Elfego Baca's Shootout

Nineteen-year-old Elfego Baca listened with mounting horror to Deputy Sheriff Pedro Sarracino's story. The deputy was from the tiny village of Frisco (present-day Reserve), but he had traveled about 130 miles east to Socorro to see Baca at the store in which he worked. Sarracino visited Socorro often, and practically every time he did, he stopped to chat with Baca. Years later Baca recalled the conversation the pair had on this day in October 1884.

> He told me that before he left Frisco for Socorro about six or seven cowboys got hold of a Mexican called "El Burro." They laid him down on the counter; one of the boys sat on his chest and arms and the other one on his lap, and that right then

and there poor Burro was altered in the presence of everybody.

Then a man by the name of Epitacio Martinez who happened to be present objected and begged them not to do that. The result was that after they were finished with Burro the same cowboys got hold of Epitacio Martinez and measured about twenty or thirty steps from where they were and tied him.

They used Epitacio as a target, and they bet drinks on who was a better shooter. Martinez was shot four different times, but still he would not die.

The deputy was afraid for his own safety. He worried that if he tried to arrest the sadistic cowboys, they would kill him, too.

Baca could not believe his ears. Although he was not above run-ins with the law himself (as a boy, he had broken his father out of jail after the elder Baca had been confined on trumped-up murder charges), he could not believe that this sworn peace officer would refuse to enforce the law. Later he described what happened next.

I told Sarracino, the deputy sheriff, that he should be ashamed of himself, having the law on his side, to permit the cowboys to do what they did. He told me that if I wanted to, I could take his job. I told him that if he would take me back to Frisco with him I would make myself a self-made deputy.

The deputy agreed, and the pair rode to Frisco. Baca pinned a mail-order badge onto his shirt and strapped on a pair of Colt .45 pistols. Then he made it known that he intended to stop the wild shooting sprees that visiting cowboys indulged in every time they came to town and got drunk. He did not have to wait long for his first test of courage.

One day in late October 1884, several dozen cowboys from the John B. Slaughter Ranch entered Frisco looking for a good time. One of them, a man named McCarty, was especially boisterous. Baca approached the drunken man, held a pistol to his head, and hauled him off to Sarracino's house, where he planned to hold him until the next day, when he could transport him to the Socorro jail.

Later in the evening, the other Slaughter cowboys demanded that Baca release McCarty. After all, who did this short, rotund Mexican with the round face and handlebar mustache think he was? They soon found out. Instead of letting McCarty go, Baca issued his own ultimatum: If the cowboys did not leave before he counted to three, he was going to open fire on them. Before the surly group could respond, Baca quickly counted to three, pulled his pistols, and commenced shooting. One of the men was thrown from his frightened horse and crushed. The rest of the rowdies retreated hastily down the street.

But the Slaughter outfit was not through with Baca. The following day Baca escorted McCarty down the street to Milligan's Bar for trial, but before he got there, he found himself surrounded by about eighty angry cowboys intent on revenge. A shot rang out from the mob, and within a split second, Baca drew both Colts. He covered the cowboys with his pistols as he ushered McCarty to the bar. After the speedy trial was over and McCarty was fined five dollars for disturbing the peace, Baca left the bar only to be confronted by the crowd of angry cowboys again.

Baca ducked into a small shack next door to the bar. Barricading himself inside, the self-proclaimed deputy sheriff prepared to fight for his life. Almost immediately the mob surrounded the shack and began firing into it. Baca fired back. His first shots pierced the roughhewn timber of the front door and cut down one of the cowboys. The others retreated in disbelief.

For the next day and a half, the well-armed cowboys tried to flush Baca from his refuge. It has been estimated that several thousand rounds of ammunition were fired into Baca's shack—four hundred into the front door alone. When the cowboys arose the second morning, hoping that Baca had died of wounds during the night, they were met by the smell of someone cooking inside the shack. Baca was making his breakfast! Unbeknownst to his attackers, he had dug a trench into the dirt floor about eighteen inches deep. He had survived by lying in this hole during the most intensive shooting, only getting up occasionally to fire a round himself.

Finally a friend talked Baca into surrendering on the condition that he could keep his weapons. Baca was then jailed in Socorro for four months on charges of murdering two of the cowboys. Later he was transported to Albuquerque for trial and was acquitted.

In later years Baca became a legitimate peace officer and a lawyer. He led an interesting and adventurous life. Then, as one of his biographers, Leon Metz, wrote,

[I]n the summer of 1945 New Mexico shook as a mushroom cloud ushered in the world's atomic age. A couple of months later, the last of the old-time gunfighters died quietly at the age of eighty.

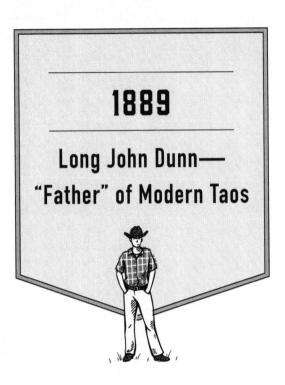

1889

Long John Dunn—
"Father" of Modern Taos

New Mexico has had its share of notable people—men and women, heroes and villains, good guys and bad guys, politicians and rascals, cowboys and American Indians—all who grace the pages of its territorial and state histories. One such person who probably was more widely known in northern New Mexico during his long and serviceable lifetime than any other citizen of the region was John Harris Dunn.

When Dunn was born in 1857, the nation stood on the brink of the Civil War. "My folks were farmers," he once related when he was nearly one hundred years old. "The love of the soil was written all over them. We were trying to make a living on a little rolling dry-land, slow-starvation farm." The Dunn family was too poor to own slaves, and all of the chores were handled by family members. Following an unsuccessful move to try his hand at farming in Missouri, Dunn's father soon moved the family back to the Waco, Texas, area just in time for him to be recruited into the Confederate Army.

Young John was only about seven years old when his broken father returned home after the war, severely wounded and in no condition to pursue the difficult chores of planting, tending, and harvesting crops. Soon afterward he died, leaving the rest of the family to face a future of abject poverty, hostile Comanche raids, and the harsh economic Reconstruction policies dictated by an unyielding and unforgiving United States government. "I dug my father's grave," Dunn lamented years later. "I tried to numb my mind to what I was doing . . . [and] I was dead set in some way I would elevate myself out of the poverty that forced me to dig my father's grave and help make his casket."

Dunn soon left his home and family in Texas and wandered about the next few years cowboying, pursuing many wild, harebrained adventures, and serving time in prison for killing a man. He soon escaped incarceration and fled to Mexico, where he learned the fine art of gambling, a trade that would be invaluable to him later in life. In 1889, at age thirty-two, he discovered Taos, New Mexico Territory, and planted his roots in the sleepy little village at the base of the Sangre de Cristo Mountains. Somewhere along the way, Dunn earned the moniker "Long" John, almost certainly because he stood about six feet four and was built like a skinny fence post.

Taos in those days was a small, mountain village that, according to the late Max Evans, noted New Mexico writer and biographer of John Dunn,

> was lifted up out of the mud. Ninety percent of its construction was of adobe, and was mud plastered. Burros, with loads of wood, and teams of wagon

horses, stood tied to the hitching posts encircling the inside of the plaza. Numerous Indians, blanketed and silent, stood watching.

Charming as Taos was to Dunn, he soon discovered that the village had no means of public transportation. A branch of the railroad dead-ended at Taos Junction, situated a few miles west of Taos, and a wooden bridge that spanned the Rio Grande connected the two towns. It seemed to Dunn that if regularly scheduled drayage service were available, it would fill a void in getting products and merchandise to the railhead for shipment beyond and allow valuable commodities to be more readily imported into northern New Mexico. Years later, in a newspaper interview, he recalled:

> I could just see myself sitting up there, with a big fine office, and my skinny stilts propped right up on top of the desk with a big black stogie shoved between my teeth. I would have stables full of good stagecoach horses, hotels, and gambling houses all over the area. It would be Long John Dunn himself that would be haulin' everybody, everywhere, and it would be Old Long John himself rakin' in the silver.

Long John attempted to purchase the bridge, but the owner priced it at $15,000, which was $11,000 more than Dunn had. He then drew upon the gambling skills that he had picked up in Mexico and along with a partner, opened two gambling venues in Taos. He also traveled around a great deal of the western United States during that period of his life, with his goal to make as much money from gambling as he could. When he returned to Taos sometime later, his pockets were swollen with $42,000.

Dunn soon ran into the bridge owner and told him that he had a potential buyer for the bridge. Apparently anxious for a quick sale this time, the owner priced the bridge at $2,200. Dunn asked the man if he would give him (Dunn) a $100 commission if he successfully sold the bridge. The owner gladly accepted the offer. The two men separated and agreed to meet again that evening at the local hotel. Together again, Dunn placed a stack of currency in the man's hand. The amazed owner counted the money and gave Dunn his commission. As he completed the bill of sale, he asked whose name should appear on it. "John Dunn. I thought it was such a bargain, I just sold it to myself."

Dunn soon discovered that two local merchants were building a competing bridge across the river at Rio Hondo, a few miles upstream from Taos. After a great deal of negotiation, the old gambler persuaded them to sell. Now, as the proud owner of two bridges, Long John was on top of the world. His daily income from the tolls charged on his bridges exceeded $200, and his gambling operations were paying off well. His joy didn't last long, however, for soon after the purchase of the second bridge, heavy snow melt in the nearby mountains turned the Rio Grande into a ravaging wall of water that destroyed both bridges.

After the flood, Dunn rounded up some workers and rebuilt the bridge at Rio Hondo. He also persuaded a high-ranking official of the Denver and Rio Grande Railroad to expand its operations in northern New Mexico. This was a monumental coup for Dunn. Tourism grew, and he built a hotel at the base of his bridge. He now owned gambling businesses in Taos, as well as other profitable enterprises. By 1898, a number of popular artists from the East were moving to Taos to establish permanent homes and studios (see "The

Birth of the Taos Art Colony" in this volume). When it was imperative for them to ship their paintings to the art shows, markets, and museums back east, Long John provided them with fast, safe service from an otherwise remote part of the West. More important, he assured that the village would soon become a worldwide mecca for art aficionados and tourists.

Eventually, John built a new home on Bent Street, where he lived the rest of his days, dying in 1953, proud of his role in the development of transportation in northern New Mexico. He often opined:

> Transportation made the West, not blazing guns as is so often preached—although I know the guns played a big part. It was those sweat-stained horses and tireless mules, those worn saddles and creaking wagons, and the men and women who were riding them across muddy rivers, rocky ridges, and up those long dusty trails.

The town of Taos and its residents owe a debt of gratitude to John Dunn. He was an entrepreneur whose far-reaching visions went a long way toward turning a small agricultural community into a premier vacation destination, as well as an international art market. Max Evans best summed up the old-timer's life when he wrote:

> John lived through three phases of the West—the gunfighting days, the cattle-working days, and the present modern West. John had come a long way, and done a lot of things since he ran away from . . . Texas, but the results of his faith in Taos as a resort and internationally-known art center will live forever.

1893

A Confrontation Between Wolf and Man

When thirty-three-year-old Ernest Thompson Seton stepped off the train at Clayton, New Mexico, on a cool, crisp day in October 1893, he was a man on a mission. The artist and naturalist had contracted with Louis Fitz-Randolph of Plainfield, New Jersey, to rid Fitz-Randolph's sprawling New Mexico ranch of depredating wolves. Fitz-Randolph had explained to Seton how productive his ranch might be if only the wolves could be kept under control. But so far, the wily animals had eluded even the best hunters and trappers. Seton, with his knowledge of animals, claimed that he was the man for the job, but as it turned out, the four weeks he gave himself to rid the L Cross F Ranch of cattle-killing wolves would not be nearly enough.

When Seton arrived in Clayton, he was weary from the five-day train ride from Chicago. He checked in at the Clayton House, rested the next day, and then hitched a ride with the local mail carrier to the ranch. The foreman and cook were away, so Seton put up at the cabin of Jim Bender, who owned a small spread nearby. Bender explained to Seton the nature of the animal he was up against. The wolves never showed themselves in the daytime—few ranch hands had even seen one—but evidence of their presence could easily be found in the trail of dead cattle they left behind after their feasts. Some local folks estimated that each wolf cost the area ranchers one thousand dollars a year.

Seton's first scheme was to poison the wolves, but after several fruitless days, it became obvious that the animals were entirely too smart for this trick. Next Seton tried trapping the wolves. He set more than one hundred steel traps, all baited with fresh meat, but every time he checked the line, he found that the wolves had sprung the traps and carried off the meat unharmed.

By January 1894, Seton was still empty-handed, and the wolves were still causing havoc among Fitz-Randolph's cattle herds. Seton was embarrassed. He had boasted of his ability to handle this job, and if he were to return to the East with no wolf kills to his credit, his reputation would suffer.

Seton soon learned from local cowhands that a pack of large wolves roamed the Currumpaw Valley about forty miles northwest of Clayton. He was intrigued by stories of a giant wolf that led this renegade pack, a big silver-haired beauty that everyone called Old Lobo. Dismayed by his monumental lack of success to date, the young naturalist decided to try his skills with the new pack. In early January 1894, he headed for the Currumpaw country.

In his autobiography, written many years after his New Mexico wolf-hunting days, Seton described the problems he had catching up with Lobo.

At the very outset, I found I could not shoot this wolf with a long-range rifle, for the very reason that I never saw him. He knew that men carry guns— against guns he could do nothing. He hid all day up in the hills, somewhere, we never knew where. But night-time he would come. And we could always tell when he was about by his voice.

Convinced that firearms were useless, Seton reverted to using poison. This method also failed. Old Lobo "merely served the baits with a wolf's contempt." Steel traps seemed to be the only answer, and Seton proceeded to set one hundred double-spring wolf traps around the countryside, each baited with fresh meat. Yet Old Lobo continued to outwit him.

As it turned out, a female wolf brought about Lobo's downfall. Blanca, a small she-wolf that appeared to be Lobo's mate, was caught one night in one of the traps. Seton used her body to mark a trail over some newly set traps, hoping to deceive Lobo into believing that his mate was still alive. Sure enough, when the men went out the following day, they found Old Lobo caught in one of the steel traps.

Seton took Lobo back to the ranch alive and attempted to feed and water him, but the old renegade would have no part of it.

"There was no wound on his body, his eye was bright and clear, he seemed in perfect health that night when I went in and left him," Seton wrote. But the next morning the naturalist found the wolf dead. "He was lying just as I had left him, his head on his paws—his muzzle down the canyon."

Old Lobo, some said, had died of a broken heart.

Seton returned to the East after his brief encounter with New Mexico's wolves and went on to become one of America's leading wildlife artists and naturalists. His books *Wild Animals I Have Known*, *Lives of the Hunted*, and *Two Little Savages*, among others, were read by millions of people worldwide. He helped found the Woodcraft League of America and the Boy Scouts of America, serving as Chief Scout from 1910 to 1915. Then, in 1930, at the height of his career and the peak of his financial independence, he moved to New Mexico and settled on twenty-five hundred acres just a few miles from Santa Fe. He retired there at Seton Castle—"on the last rampart of the Rockies, in the land where still the Indian lives unchanged, and where the Buffalo Wind is blowing; where the Rio Grande rolls as it always has, through unchanged mountains and realms of snow, to its rest in the far-off sea."

He died there in 1946 at the age of eighty-six.

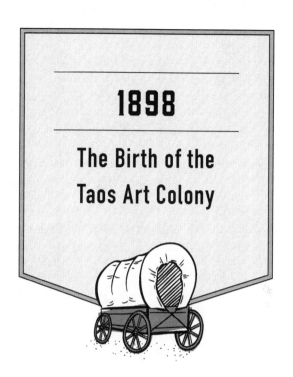

1898

The Birth of the Taos Art Colony

On the afternoon of September 3, 1898, two young men rattled southward in a horse-drawn wagon, headed from Denver to Taos, New Mexico. They were greenhorn artists from the East, and their mission was to set up a studio in Taos where they could spend a few weeks painting the sights of the northern New Mexican countryside.

One of the artists, Ernest Blumenschein, was a twenty-four-year-old native of Pittsburgh, Pennsylvania, although he had grown up in Ohio. The son of an eminent musician, he had been commissioned by *McClure's* magazine to travel to the Southwest on a sketching trip. This trek to Taos was the last leg of his journey.

Blumenschein's traveling companion was thirty-year-old Bert Phillips, a New York native who, like Blumenschein, had trained at the exclusive Julien Academy in Paris. The pair had briefly shared a studio in New York City until Blumenschein's magazine commission prompted them to pull up stakes and head west.

As the creaky covered wagon lumbered down the rock-strewn road through the southern Sangre de Cristo Mountains, Blumenschein and Phillips marveled at the beauty that surrounded them. What a wonderful place to paint, they thought. It was every bit as breathtaking as their artist friend Joseph Sharp had told them. Sharp had visited Taos in 1893 and had written and illustrated a popular article about his trip for *Harper's Weekly* magazine. When he later met Blumenschein and Phillips at the Julien Academy, he enthralled the younger men with tales of the area's mystique.

For a few more moments, the wagon bumped along. In it were art supplies, food, clothing—in short, just about everything the two struggling artists owned. So far the journey had been interesting but nerve-racking. Phillips later wrote that

> it was before the days of automobiles, wagon roads were bad; bridges in southern Colorado and northern New Mexico were made of loose poles laid across the log stringers, often over deep arroyos, these poles rolled and sprung under the horses' feet. We expected every minute to see their legs break in their effort, our sighs of relief were audible when we were safely across. We began to realize that a kind Providence was with us for in spite of a smashed wheel ... repairs at every blacksmith's shop we passed; our last dollar spent, we reached our destination—Taos.

It was then that the last in a long line of mishaps occurred. As the wagon rolled over a large rock in the middle of the road, one of the wheels slipped off the axle and rolled down a nearby embankment. The two tired men did not know what to do. A quick inspection convinced them that they could not fix the wheel, and there was no sign of a blacksmith nearby. So, they decided that one of them would ride down the mountain to Taos on horseback to get the wheel repaired, while the other man waited behind to guard the wagon and its contents.

To decide which would make the arduous trip, the two men flipped a three-dollar gold piece. Blumenschein lost. He later wrote:

> I started down the mountain on what resulted in the most impressive journey of my life. It took me until dark to reach the foot of this long hill. There I spent the night with a hospitable Spanish-American farmer— one dollar for frijoles, bed, and frijoles again for breakfast. It was early in the morning when I resumed the horseback ride. My muscles soon ached from carrying the broken wheel. What had seemed a simple job when we tossed the coin, had become a painful task.... Vividly I recall the discomfort with no relief in sight on the road, no wagon going my way, no hope to ease sore muscles until I reached Taos, a dim picture of which I had made from Sharp's slight description.

Blumenschein's uncomfortable trip to Taos opened an entirely new chapter in his life. He was overwhelmed by the beauty of the countryside. "No artist had ever recorded the superb New Mexico I was now seeing," he later wrote. "I was receiving ... the first great unforgettable inspiration of my life."

Blumenschein had the wheel fixed and carried it back up the mountain. Then he and Phillips rolled into Taos, rented an adobe house, and converted it into a combination studio and home. September soon passed, and it was time to return to the East. But Phillips decided to stay in Taos permanently. Blumenschein went home to Pittsburgh, but he returned regularly to visit until 1919 when he moved to Taos for the rest of his life.

Caught in the spell of this Land of Enchantment, Blumenschein and Phillips soon lured friends and fellow painters to Taos with stories of the region's peace and beauty. By 1912 the two men, along with four of their colleagues, had formally created the Taos Society of Artists, one of the foremost artists' groups in the nation. In the decades since then, Taos has remained a magnet not only for talented artists, but for great writers such as D. H. Lawrence as well.

1898

The Birth of the Rough Riders

In mid-February 1898, New Mexico Territorial Governor Miguel A. Otero received word in Santa Fe that Spanish troops had sunk the battleship USS *Maine* in the harbor at Havana, Cuba. The news concerned Otero because New Mexico, although a U.S. territory for more than fifty years, was largely inhabited by people of Spanish descent. He, himself, was one of them, born in Saint Louis and educated at Notre Dame. He felt a twinge of sorrow when he read the report.

Otero had no doubt what course of action he must follow. He must make sure no one could question the loyalty of the people of New Mexico. He promptly wrote to the *New York World* that, "in anticipation of War, the New Mexico National guard, in many localities, are drilling night and day." In early

April the governor advised U.S. Secretary of War R. A. Alger that "a full regiment of cavalry, nearly all of whom are of Spanish descent," was ready for immediate service.

Men volunteered for service in growing numbers until, on April 24, the *Santa Fe New Mexican* could proudly proclaim in its headlines:

> Volunteers Galore. Offers For Active Service Pouring In On Governor Otero From All Over New Mexico. Recruiting The Maximum. National Guards Ready On Call Two Thousand Men Could Be Had On Short Notice.

On April 25, the federal government officially declared war on Spain, reacting to Spain's own declaration of war the previous day. Alger advised Otero of the action by telegram and added:

> The president directs that Captain Leonard Wood, United States army, be authorized to raise a regiment of cavalry as mounted riflemen, and to be its colonel and has named Hon. Theodore Roosevelt as lieutenant colonel. All of the other officers will come from the vicinity where the troops are raised. What can you do for them? Answer immediately.

Without delay, Otero wired his response:

> Telegram arrived. Have full squadron of cavalry ready for service. Prefer to send them as cavalrymen, but probably can transfer as mounted riflemen, if necessary. Can raise battalion of mounted riflemen in about a week. Can you take squadron of cavalry and battalion of mounted riflemen in addition?

The next day Secretary Alger informed Otero that the New Mexican volunteers would be used as mounted riflemen under the command of Colonel Wood. Anticipating a mad rush to join the ranks of such an illustrious organization, the *Santa Fe New Mexican* reported on April 28 that

[t]he four troops of mounted riflemen being organized in New Mexico for service in Cuba, will in many respects be the most noted volunteer squadron ever enlisted. Every man is to be picked with reference to special qualifications. He must be a good shot, be able to ride anything in the line of horseflesh, a rough and ready fighter, and above all must absolutely have no understanding of the word fear. . . . To belong to New Mexico's mounted riflemen as a private is an honor which will be looked upon as beyond that of a commissioned officer in many another organization.

The response to the call to arms was as expected. Scores of New Mexicans volunteered their services, and when the final tally was in, 340 of the territory's finest had reported for duty in the First Volunteer Cavalry Regiment, which also included men from Arizona, Oklahoma, and Indian Territories. The New Mexican contingent was the largest in the regiment and was commanded by Adjutant General Henry Hersey.

The volunteers were equipped and armed by the federal government. One of the troop commander's, Captain T. P. Ledwidge, described the typical soldier's gear in a letter to the *Denver Republican.*

Each man is supplied with a McClellan saddle, bridle, water bridle, halter, saddlebags . . . picket pin and rope, nose bag, curry comb and brush, spurs, canteen, mess pan and tin cup, knife, fork and spoon, poncho, body blanket, horse blanket, one-half shelter tent, service belt, machete and scabbard, Krag-Jorgensen 30-30 carbine and scabbard, 44-caliber single action Colt's revolver and scabbard and cartridge belt.

By the time the volunteers reached San Antonio, Texas, where a training and staging area had been established, they were being called by a variety of names, including the Cowboy Cavalry, the Fighting First, Teddy's Riotous Rounders, and the name that eventually stuck with them, the Rough Riders. Although he learned to accept the moniker, Roosevelt at first was hesitant to call his military cohorts by any such name. "Don't call them rough riders and don't call them cowboys," he exclaimed. "Call them mounted riflemen."

Roosevelt, who had served as undersecretary of the Navy before resigning to help organize the Volunteers, was unwavering in his high regard for the New Mexicans. He once described them as "a splendid set of men . . . tall and sinewy, with resolute, weather-beaten faces, and eyes that looked a man straight in the face without flinching."

After training, the Volunteers departed for Cuba, landing there on June 22. Two days later the Rough Riders got their first taste of combat when, with Lieutenant Colonel Roosevelt in command, they won a decisive battle at Las Guasimas.

"Every officer and man did his duty up to the handle," exclaimed a proud Roosevelt. On July 1 and 2, the Rough Riders helped the U.S. Army to occupy the San Juan Heights, and on August 7, after Spain had sued for peace, the men of New Mexico returned home.

On August 25 Roosevelt wrote Governor Otero a letter expressing his thanks for the territory's cooperation in the war effort. "I write you a line just to tell you how admirable the New Mexican troopers ... have behaved," he wrote. "I am more than proud to be in the same regiment with them; I can imagine no greater honor than to have commanded such men."

1901

Black Jack Ketchum
Meets His Maker

Thomas Ketchum, a giant of a man with a striking black handlebar mustache, sat dejectedly in his jail cell in Clayton, New Mexico. For several days he had watched from his cell window as workmen put the finishing touches on the gallows that he knew would be used for his own hanging. From time to time, Ketchum would yell at the busy men outside. According to a *New York Times* reporter, the prisoner dryly remarked on the day before his scheduled execution, "Very good, boys, but why don't you tear down that stockade so the boys can see a man hang who never killed a man?"

Ketchum, known to the press as "Black Jack," had been in confinement since his arrest in August 1899, following an attempted train holdup near Folsom, New Mexico. This marked the third time in two years that the "Texas Express," a train on the Colorado and Southern line, had been stopped by Black Jack or members of his gang. Each time, Frank E. Harrington had been on board as the conductor.

On the third occasion, Ketchum had attempted the robbery by himself. When Harrington realized that his train was being held up, he grabbed a shotgun and made his way to the front of the train. Later he explained that

> [i]n the dim light I plainly saw the robber who moved quickly about exhorting four trainmen who were his prisoners to do his bidding. The men were perhaps ten feet from me, the trainmen standing close together in line with the bandit.

Harrington recognized Ketchum from the outlaw's previous holdups. As the conductor raised his shotgun, Black Jack caught a glimpse of him out of the corner of his eye. Both men fired at about the same time, and both were wounded in the arm. Harrington wrote:

> I'd have killed him if he'd waited a fraction of a second. I had a bead on his heart but his buckshot jiggled my aim. . . . I wanted to hit the bandit in the heart, but in the dim light I misjudged. It had to be done quickly. I knew that as I opened the door my appearance would be noted by the robber, who faced me. I aimed as best as I could.

After the gunplay Harrington dressed his nicked arm, while Ketchum jumped off the train. Sheriff's deputies found him the next day, lying beside the railroad tracks and bleeding profusely from eleven buckshot wounds in his right arm.

Union County Sheriff Saturnino Pinard and his men took Ketchum to Folsom for medical care. From there he was taken to Trinidad, Colorado, for questioning and then to Santa Fe. All the while he maintained that he was George Stevens and not Thomas "Black Jack" Ketchum. However, a former sheriff from San Angelo, Texas, positively identified the tall train robber.

Arizona authorities wanted to extradite Ketchum and try him for the murder of two shopkeepers in Camp Verde. However, New Mexico Governor Miguel Otero refused the request and ordered that Black Jack be tried under a recently enacted territorial law that provided the death penalty for "molesting a train." Ketchum was moved first to Las Vegas, then to Clayton, where he was tried in the handsome, two-story, red-brick Victorian courthouse.

As expected, Black Jack pleaded not guilty to the train robbery charge. However, the jury was unconvinced. It returned a guilty verdict, and Judge William J. Mills sentenced Ketchum to hang on October 5, 1900. Because of an appeal and other postponements, the execution was delayed until April 26, 1901.

On that afternoon a crowd of curious onlookers gathered around the gallows, straining to get a glimpse of the handsome and notorious train robber. This would be the first official hanging ever witnessed in Clayton, and space was so scarce that admission to the spectacle was permitted by ticket only. Witnesses recalled later that, as he left his jail cell, Ketchum literally ran to the gallows in the jail yard, almost as if he were anxious to get done with the gruesome act. As deputies placed the hood over Ketchum's head and the noose around his neck, Sheriff Salome Garcia asked Black Jack if he had any last words.

"Ready, let her go," replied Ketchum.

Garcia released the trap door, and Ketchum's heavy body dropped through the opening. The crowd had turned to leave when a woman shouted that blood was seeping from under the hood. When officials removed it, they found to their horror that Ketchum's head had almost been ripped from his body by the intense weight of his fall.

Black Jack Ketchum went to his grave denying his identity. Nevertheless, Clayton authorities were convinced they had executed the right man. The unclaimed body was buried on the outskirts of town and lay there until 1933, when it was exhumed and moved to another cemetery.

1908

The Mysterious Demise of Pat Garrett

More than a quarter of a century had passed since Pat Garrett had catapulted into the national spotlight for killing Billy the Kid. Now, in 1908, he was an embittered man. Still strikingly handsome, the fifty-eight-year-old Garrett whose six-foot, four-inch frame towered over most of his acquaintances pulled himself onto the seat of a buckboard that was about to set out for Las Cruces, New Mexico. His mission was to attempt to settle a dispute over the lease of part of his ranch to Wayne Brazel. Garrett's son, Poe, had done the actual leasing, and when Pat had found out that Brazel was grazing almost two thousand goats on the land, he had become furious.

In the meantime, James B. Miller, a noted gunman, along with one of his relatives, Carl Adamson, had offered to buy the land in question from Garrett, provided the goats were removed. When the goat problem could not be readily resolved, Garrett decided to have a meeting of all parties concerned and bring the matter to a conclusion.

So it was that on February 29, 1908, Garrett and Adamson left the ranch near Organ and began the twelve-mile trip to Las Cruces to the meeting that Garrett hoped would bring him out of the debt he had found himself in for the past several years. About a mile or so down the road, the pair met Brazel riding horseback to the meeting. For the next few miles, the threesome rode along together, exchanging words now and then despite their strained relations.

Near a dry streambed called Alameda Arroyo, Adamson stopped to relieve himself. Garrett jumped out of the buckboard to do likewise. As he stood behind the wagon, a pistol shot reverberated across the countryside, then another. Garrett had been shot twice, once in the head, and his body crumpled to the earth. Leaving Garrett lying in the road, Brazel and Adamson continued on to Las Cruces, where they reported the killing to the sheriff. Brazel admitted firing the shots but insisted that he had done so in self-defense, despite the coroner's findings that the fatal shot had entered the back of Garrett's head.

A team of investigators—including the governor, the attorney general, and the captain of the territorial mounted police—concluded that despite Brazel's confession, someone else had killed Garrett. Nevertheless, Brazel was indicted, tried, and eventually acquitted of the murder. Today there are several theories about who really killed Garrett. Some of the suspects include Miller, Adamson, and even Print Rhode, Brazel's partner in the goat venture. The truth is, no one knows for sure.

When Garrett died on that lonely road to Las Cruces in 1908, the books closed on one of the most romantic episodes in Western history. Garrett had been one of the last old-time sheriffs to enforce the law in the wild Southwest when the most notorious outlaws still rode. He is best known for shooting and killing Billy the Kid at Fort Sumner in 1881.

But Garrett was more than just a good law enforcement officer. He was a good businessman as well, and he was quick to recognize a potential moneymaker when he saw one. Fewer than nine months after he killed the Kid, Garrett—probably assisted by a fifty-three-year-old New Mexican journalist named Ash Upson—published a book describing the entire incident, as well as providing background information on Billy's life. Entitled *The Authentic Life of Billy, the Kid, the Noted Desperado of the Southwest, Whose Deeds of Daring and Blood Made his Name a Terror in New Mexico, Arizona & Northern Mexico*, the book, despite its frequent flights from the truth, is one of the most popular ever written about the Kid and is still in print today.

Garrett set the stage for his narrative in the opening paragraph of his introduction. He wrote:

> Yielding to repeated solicitations from various sources, I have addressed myself to the task of compiling, for publication, a true history of the life, adventures, and tragic death of William H. Bonney, better known as "Billy the Kid," whose daring deeds and bloody crimes have excited, for some years past, the wonder of one-half of the world, and the admiration or detestation of the other half.

After the initial success of his book, Garrett dabbled in New Mexican politics, promoted an irrigation project in the

Pecos River valley, moved to Texas, returned to New Mexico, took up the badge again, and finally, in 1901, was appointed by President Theodore Roosevelt to the post of collector of customs in El Paso, Texas. Four years later, when his appointment expired, a miffed Roosevelt refused to renew it because Garrett had arranged for a photograph to be taken of himself, the president, and a man named Tom Powers at the 1905 Rough Riders Reunion in San Antonio, Texas. Roosevelt found out too late to spare him a great deal of public embarrassment that Powers was not a large ranch owner, as Garrett had intimated, but rather the owner of the notorious Coney Island Saloon in El Paso.

At the time of Garrett's murder, the once-respected lawman was practically destitute. Except for his modest ranch near Organ, he had nothing. Indeed the disputed ownership of the ranch, along with the problem that Garrett was journeying to Las Cruces to resolve, more than likely figured prominently in his strange demise.

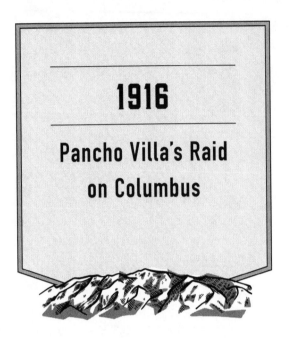

1916

Pancho Villa's Raid on Columbus

Sergeant Ellery Waters of "C" Troop, Thirteenth Cavalry, was on guard duty early on March 9, 1916, patrolling the small army garrison at Columbus, New Mexico, about two miles north of the Mexican border. A couple of days earlier, Colonel H. J. Slocum, the commanding officer of the garrison, had been advised that the Mexican revolutionary and bandit Pancho Villa had been sighted in the area with a large force of armed horsemen. Villa, in his continuous attempt to usurp control of the Mexican government from his archrival President Venustiano Carranza, had for years maintained an on-again, off-again relationship with American authorities. Although he had killed several American citizens in the past, his possible presence this day caused no undue fear among the tough and hardened veterans of the Thirteenth Cavalry.

Shortly after 2:30 a.m., Waters completed his last inspection before breakfast. As he headed his horse, Eagle, toward "C" Troop's encampment, he was suddenly confronted by dozens of shouting, shooting Mexicans riding through the streets of Columbus. In the distance he could hear the rapid burping of a machine gun. Waters, a fourteen-year veteran of the cavalry, had seen service in the Philippines during the savage insurrection there earlier in the century. He knew enemy fire when he heard it, and within an instant, he had drawn his new-issue 1911 .45 Colt automatic and fired three clips into the throng of horsemen.

In the meantime, on the other side of town, a young Army lieutenant had only hours earlier returned from El Paso, Texas, where a large number of officers of the Thirteenth Cavalry were on leave playing polo. The soldier had just assumed his duties when he heard a shot, looked outside, and saw an enlisted man on guard duty fall dead. He shot and killed the Mexican horseman responsible for the deed. As he ran outside, he was met with screams from scores of mounted Mexicans shouting "¡Viva Villa! ¡Viva Mexico! ¡Muerte a los americanos!"

Hysterical civilians ran helplessly into the streets. James Dean, whom everyone knew as the friendly and accommodating grocer, was shot in his tracks as he crossed Main Street. When the Richie Hotel caught on fire, its owner ran into the street and begged for his life. After giving the Villistas every cent he had on him, fifty dollars, he was shot and killed anyway. Mrs. Wright, an eyewitness to the attack who only minutes before had been freed by the Mexican army, which had taken her captive a few days earlier, remarked: "I did not know I could have such hate in my heart. I saw

Mexicans horribly wounded and suffering terribly and did not care how much they suffered."

Bullets flew everywhere, and as more and more of the men of the Thirteenth Cavalry became involved in the fight, the Villistas prepared to retreat across the international border. When the smoke cleared and casualties were counted, it was determined that six U.S. soldiers and nine civilians had been killed. During the two-hour raid, the Villistas had also destroyed the railroad station and two other buildings, looted three stores, and stolen seven cavalry horses. They had lost fifty men in Columbus, and seventy more would die the following day as the Thirteenth Cavalry pursued them into Mexico.

Mexico's new president, Venustiano Carranza, officially apologized to the United States for the attack on Columbus. He vowed to "use the most vigorous means to run this man [Villa] to earth and avenge his horrible acts." Citizens everywhere were shocked that such an atrocity could happen on U.S. soil and right under the noses of several crack troops of cavalry. In Washington, D.C., President Woodrow Wilson fretted over what to do as he read in the press of the growing outrage of the American people. The *New York Tribune* issued a scathing criticism of the president, declaring that "the Bryan-Wilson policy . . . of dodging the duty of protecting them [American citizens] when living, and of avenging them when dead, has borne its perfect fruit." The angry publishing magnate, William Randolph Hearst, wrote:

> California and Texas were part of Mexico once. . . .
> What has been done in California and Texas by the
> United States can be done ALL THE WAY DOWN
> TO THE SOUTHERN BANK OF THE PANAMA

CANAL. . . . Our flag should wave over Mexico as the symbol of the rehabilitation of that unhappy country and its redemption to humanity and civilization.

U.S. authorities considered their political and military options and even advertised for fifty-four trucks to accompany a punitive expedition south of the border. Finally, on March 15, nearly one week after the violence at Columbus, General John J. Pershing and a force that would eventually approach fifteen thousand soldiers rode into Mexico with orders to find Pancho Villa. At their disposal were motor cars, trucks, and eight airplanes.

After nearly a year of chasing Villa across the arid deserts and canyon lands of northern Mexico, Pershing and his tired, haggard men returned to the United States empty-handed. The Americans had fought several engagements with Villa's men, killing many in the process. But the primary object of their mission, Pancho Villa, had eluded them. About all that the punitive expedition had accomplished was to provide combat training for Pershing and his troops that would later prove invaluable when the United States entered World War I. And it was the first time that the new army sidearm, the 1911 Colt .45 automatic pistol, was used extensively in combat, thus assuring it a place in American military history. On the downside the expedition had cost U.S. taxpayers $130 million and had yielded no recompense for the people murdered at Columbus, New Mexico, on that March day in 1916.

1929

Weird Happenings in Taos

On July 4, 1929, Taoseños were a little rattled when they learned that one of their neighbors, a seldom-seen, much disliked recluse, had been murdered the day before in his sprawling mansion on Paseo del Pueblo Norte. The brief but graphic description in the *Taos News* mundanely reported that the man's "body [was] found in a mutilate condition and his head severed from his body." To most residents, the shock came not from the fact that the man was killed by an intruder but that his homicide had been carried out with such brutality.

Murder and mayhem were not new to the people of the Land of Enchantment. New Mexico historian and educator George Sánchez wrote in his 1940 book, *Forgotten People*:

The people of Taos have [always] been a restless people. Far removed from the center of government in colonial days, they have long been accustomed to the independence of the frontier. That independence and restlessness has often been manifested— in the search for lands, in conflicts with the Indians, in dealings with the authorities of government. Probably no section of the state has witnessed as many revolts, plots, and counterplots, as have been staged in Taos.

Beginning with the Pueblo Revolt of 1680, which drove the early Spanish invaders back south to Santa Fe and beyond, Taoseños had also witnessed the Chimayo Rebellion of 1837 and the brutal Taos Revolt and Insurrection ten years later. So, indeed, although violence and bloodshed were no strangers to the residents of early twentieth-century Taos and the surrounding region, the method of this particular murder was decidedly bizarre and kept people talking for a long time.

The victim was identified as Arthur Rochford Manby. The backstory of Manby's strange case goes back all the way to 1883 when he first appeared in Taos and, with a thick English accent, announced to the townsfolks that he was to be their newest neighbor. The short, stocky, twenty-four-year-old presented himself rather agreeably, dressed in a neatly pressed white dress shirt, tie, and a smart business suit complete with vest. However, based on their past history with intruders, the folks of Taos had ample reason to be leery of a tight-lipped European newcomer who acted like royalty.

For the first few years, Manby was an elusive character around town. He kept his distance, and folks had a hard time learning much about where he had come from and why he suddenly had shown up in their remote village. Eventually, they might have discovered that he was the eighth-born child of a British churchman and his wife, an artist. He had studied mineralogy and architecture in school and, shortly after graduation, when he read about the untold riches of America's western frontier, he set sail for New York City in 1883, arriving in New Mexico later in the year.

For the first few years after his arrival in Taos, Manby kept himself busy investigating land grants and gold mining properties in the region. He was a smooth-talking, master con man who gleefully bilked American Indians and New Mexicans alike out of their land and their mines. He even swindled wealthy Eastern investors into financially backing his efforts. Mary Hunzicker Dunn, a director of the Taos Center for the Arts, wrote that the scheming Manby

> was characterized as having a brilliant mind, refined taste, and an appreciation of the visual beauty of the Taos Valley, on the one hand, yet he was devious, calculating, greedy, manipulating, persistent, and a murderer. In short, he was a loner, and had few if any friends in Taos.

In 1898, Manly decided to erect a massive mansion in Taos, and the property upon which he chose to build it ran north along the east side of Paseo del Pueblo Norte between the present-day Taos Inn/Doc Martin's Restaurant establishments and Kit Carson Park. Nine years later, upon completion, the hacienda contained nineteen rooms, all splendidly furnished with the finest furniture and appointments that money (most likely someone else's) could buy.

In 1913, now in his mid-fifties, Manby somehow acquired nearly fifty-nine thousand acres of the huge Antonio Martinez land grant located nearby. But, by then, his harebrained con schemes were no longer providing the cash flow he needed to keep his many projects viable. Three years later, he lost the land grant, which left him in tremendous debt and with only the Taos hacienda under his control.

Over the years, Manby's strange and inexplicable behavior around town worsened. His almost half century residence in Taos came to a tragic and bizarre end in early July 1929 when two law enforcement officers found his decapitated body in a front room of his home, which was swarming with flies. The victim's mutilated head was located in a second room, along with his frightened dog. In those days, before forensics and DNA analysis played such roles in criminal investigation as they do today, Manby's demise was quickly ruled a "death by natural causes." The dog most likely separated the head from the body, according to the report. Manby was buried on his property on the same day.

The horrific news quickly spread. Sometime later, when Manby's family in England and the British consulate in Galveston began inquiring into the death, New Mexico's governor ordered that the body be exhumed and an autopsy performed. Longtime resident and Manby's next-door neighbor, Dr. T. P. (Doc) Martin; Dr. Fred Muller, Manby's dentist; H. D. Martin, a detective dispatched to the scene by the New Mexico attorney general; and others reviewed the evidence and identified the corpse as Manby's. They declared that the Englishman had been shot multiple times and that his head had not been chewed off by the dog, but it had been deliberately severed from the neck. The body was reburied and the investigation eventually was suspended, no doubt because

Dr. Muller soon retracted his earlier testimony, and Doc Martin reportedly disposed of the autopsy findings.

On February 25, 1930, Detective Martin wrote a letter to New Mexico governor R. C. Dillon in which he declared that Manby was murdered in cold blood, motivated by "robbery, jealousy, fear and vengeance." Martin named four local suspects as the culprits, adding, "I do not see any mystery in the A. R. Manby case. If less publicity, less talk, and more work was done, the guilty . . . could be brought to justice without much time." However, the Manby investigation became a cold case and apparently remains so today.

Following Manby's death, Dr. Victor C. Thorne, one of the wealthy investors from New York City he had bilked, foreclosed on the mortgage that he held on Manby's Taos hacienda. By then, according to Mary H. Dunn, "all of Manby's possessions and treasures [had] mysteriously disappeared," and "the roof had fallen in, windows were broken, and squatters inhabited some rooms." Dr. Thorne financed the complete restoration of the building, complete with central heating, which was the first such installation in Taos. When Dr. Thorne died in 1948, a trust fund—the Taos Foundation—managed the property; four years later, the Taos Artists' Association purchased the house and three acres. For the next seventy years—and counting—the structure has provided homes to many organizations, including the present-day occupants, the Taos Center for the Arts.

1937

The Penitent Brotherhood

A t dusk on Good Friday 1937, several men of Hispanic origin gathered inside a small church in the mountains of northern New Mexico. They were members of Los Hermanos Penitentes, the Penitent Brothers, a religious sect dating back at least a century. It probably evolved from customs of the conquistadors who frequented the region during the sixteenth century.

As the Brothers took their places, the church slowly filled with men, women, and children from the neighborhood. They huddled in the tiny sanctuary, trying to fend off the springtime chill, as someone lit candles and closed the windows and doors. Long shadows climbed the adobe walls, and brilliantly painted religious icons peered down at the well-mannered crowd.

When all were ready, the Brothers began to perform a ceremony called Tinieblas, a re-creation of the earthquake that was said to unsettle Calvary at the moment of Christ's death. As the candles were extinguished one by one, symbolizing the darkness that fell across the land, the crowd began to wail, and the men of the Brotherhood began to whip themselves with yucca cords. Then all the participants filed out of the church into the stillness of the night.

Now the ceremony had reached its climax. The chief Brother, or Hermano Mayor, stepped out of the crowd and hoisted a large wooden cross that lay on the ground outside the church. As the man dragged the heavy cross to a predetermined spot several hundred yards away, he was followed by several other Brothers, some quietly reading from prayer books, some accompanying the carreta del muerto, or wagon of death, and others bearing crosses upon their backs as well. The rest of the Brothers, called flagellants, wore cloth masks over their heads and whipped themselves continuously until blood oozed from their backs and legs.

A spectator, writer Alice Corbin Henderson, later described the procession:

> The rhythmic stroke of the yucca lash came down ... on dripping backs, the heavy lash lifted with both hands and swung first over one shoulder and then the other; then a few steps taken, and another stroke of the lash. Not—in spite of the spectacular sight of blood—so severe a penance as some others. The next single penitent was a man of extraordinary powerful build, his entire torso tightly bound with branching cactus ... and his ankles shackled with heavy, dragging iron chains.

Marching to the eerie tune of a flute and in the flickering light of scores of candles, the men finally reached their destination, the Calvario, or place of Calvary. One of the Brothers was tightly lashed to the largest of the crosses. He grimaced in pain as it was lifted upright. When he lost consciousness, thus imitating the death of Christ, he was cut down from the cross and carried back to the church to recover.

Legend has it that in times past, many Brothers who played the part of Christ failed to survive their ordeal and were buried at the spot on which they died. Each of their graves was marked by a cross and a pile of stones. Even today, as one drives the back roads of New Mexico—among the villages of Truchas, Taos, Mora, San Miguel, Chimayo, and others in the counties of Rio Arriba, Colfax, and Valencia—one can see vestiges of these crosses and stone cairns scattered across the countryside.

Although the Catholic Church officially denounced the Brotherhood, its edicts did little to curtail the popularity of the movement in rural New Mexico. As early as 1833, the bishop of Durango forbade

for all time to come those brotherhoods of penitence—or, better still, of Butchery—which have been growing under the shelter of inexcusable toleration. Each parish-priest, or friar-minister, in all the territory of this administration, will see to it that not a single one of those brotherhoods remains in existence.... Moderate penance is not forbidden ... but let it be performed without assemblages wrongly called brotherhoods which have no legal authorization whatsoever.

The bishop's directive did little good. When Josiah Gregg, the "father of the Santa Fe Trail," wrote his book *Commerce of the Prairies* in 1844, the Brothers were still active. Gregg noted that he "once chanced to be in the town of Tome on Good Friday, when my attention was arrested by a man almost naked, bearing . . . a huge cross upon his shoulders, which . . . must have weighed over a hundred pounds."

It is doubtful that the Easter ritual of the Penitent Brothers still results in the deaths of members today. But it is almost a certainty that, way back in the rural recesses of the Sangre de Cristo Mountains of northern New Mexico and southern Colorado, the Brotherhood still exists, observing the Easter season with its age-old traditions.

1945

Countdown at Trinity

At two o'clock on the morning of July 16, 1945, several busloads of anxious spectators pulled up to a scenic overlook about sixty miles northwest of Alamogordo, New Mexico. A few months earlier the U.S. Army had leased this entire region, including the ranch of David McDonald. Just exactly what the army planned to do with it would be revealed in less than four hours, when the visitors, mostly scientists and workers from Los Alamos, New Mexico, would witness the explosion of the world's first atomic bomb.

As the crowd waited for the final minutes of the countdown, the suspense must have been overwhelming. One observer remarked, "With the darkness and the waiting in the chill of the desert the tension became almost unendurable." At 5:25 a.m., five minutes before the atomic device was set to explode, a warning rocket spewing green smoke was sent up. Four minutes later, another rocket was fired, signifying that only sixty seconds remained before detonation. When the spectators were told to lie face down in the sand, Edward Teller, a Hungarian-born physicist who had immigrated to the United States in the 1930s and who was one of the developers of the atomic bomb, would have no part of it. He wrote later that he was

> determined to look the beast in the eye. I put on a pair of dark glasses. I pulled on a pair of heavy gloves. With both hands I pressed the welder's glass to my face, making sure no stray light could penetrate around it. I then looked straight at the aim point.

What happened next at the Trinity Site, as "ground zero" for the explosion was named, is best described by another eyewitness:

> At "minus 45 seconds" a robot mechanism took over the controls. Suddenly a giant ball of fire rose as though from the bowels of the earth, then a pillar of purple fire, 10,000 feet high, shooting skyward. Its bottom was brown, its center was amber; its top, white. The flash lit up every crevasse and ridge of the San Andres Mountains. Then it shot higher, to 40,000 feet, a huge, rainbow-colored ball, turning swiftly to mushroom shape. It was lit from within by lightning like flashes. There was a tremendous sustained roar. In Albuquerque, 120 miles away, the sky blazed noonday-bright. When it was done, the tower [that held the bomb] had completely vaporized. There was only a crater a quarter-mile wide lined with melted rock and sand.

One of Teller's scientist friends who also observed the explosion later wrote:

> At the instant of the explosion I was looking directly at it, with no eye protection of any kind. I saw first a yellow glow, which grew almost instantly to an overwhelming white flash, so intense that I was completely blinded. . . . By twenty or thirty seconds after the explosion I was regaining normal vision. . . . The grandeur and magnitude of the phenomenon were completely breathtaking.

The countdown at Trinity had begun years earlier, when the German-American physicist, Albert Einstein, already aware of Nazi research into atomic physics, suggested to President Franklin D. Roosevelt that the United States immerse itself in the study of nuclear fission. On December 6, 1941, the day before the Japanese attacked Pearl Harbor, Roosevelt signed the order that plunged the United States into the largest single enterprise in the history of science to date, the ultrasecret "Manhattan Project." General Leslie Groves was placed in charge of the project, and Robert Oppenheimer was chosen to lead the development and production of an atomic bomb.

One of the first tasks facing General Groves was the identification and acquisition of a suitable site for an atomic laboratory. According to Richard Rhodes, in his book, *The Making of the Atomic Bomb*, the site had to provide "room for 265 people, location at least two hundred miles from any international boundary but west of the Mississippi, some existing facilities, a natural bowl with hills nearby that shaped the bowl so that fences might be strung on top and guarded."

After two other sites were rejected, one in Utah and the other near Jemez Springs, New Mexico, a third possibility was surveyed and accepted. The chosen location was the site of a boys' school called the Los Alamos Ranch School. It sat atop a 7,200-foot mesa, a far cry from the "natural bowl" originally specified by Groves. Nevertheless, when the general saw the site for the first time in late 1942, he said, "This is the place." A Corps of Engineers appraisal, prepared in November 1942, showed that the school and its properties including two trucks, fifty saddles, sixty horses, twenty-five tons of coal, sixteen hundred books, and eight hundred cords of firewood were worth nearly $450,000. The school administrator agreed to accept that price, and the Los Alamos Ranch School became the Los Alamos National Laboratory.

From late 1942 until the atomic-bomb prototype was exploded at the Trinity Site in July 1945, scores of scientists worked behind high walls and in absolute security at the Los Alamos Laboratory. It was here that the top-secret atomic bomb design was developed. And it was here as well that the various components were assembled into the bomb itself.

Today the Los Alamos National Laboratory is still functional, and nuclear research continues there, although most of the study is for peaceful purposes. The Trinity Site is part of the White Sands Missile Range and is open to the public two times a year.

1947

The Curious Incident
at Roswell

A side from the temperature being a little cooler as a result of a severe storm the previous night, the morning of July 3, 1947, dawned much like any other in this remote section of dry prairie near Corona, New Mexico. William "Mac" Brazel, a foreman on the Foster Ranch, rose earlier than normal that day to check for any damage to the large sheep spread that might have been caused by the violent weather. As he jumped into his pickup, Brazel was joined by his constant companion, a seven-year-old neighbor boy named Dee Proctor.

After the pair left ranch headquarters, they drove for several minutes in silence, each carefully observing the terrain and the livestock for damages. When they did begin to talk, the subject quickly turned to the strange noises they had heard during the night. Fully expecting to find the remains of a light airplane, or perhaps even a helicopter, the pair became somewhat frustrated when several hours of searching turned up nothing.

Toward noon Brazel and the boy spied something bright and shiny in a pasture and went to investigate. As they drew nearer, they noticed that pieces of a peculiar, metallic-looking substance resembling aluminum foil were strewn over the pasture for several yards in all directions. Mixed in with the metallic material were other pieces of debris made from a substance that resembled modern-day plastic.

Forty-three years later, Dee Proctor's mother, Loretta, recalled her first impression of the materials. According to her,

> [T]he piece . . . looked like a kind of tan, light-brown plastic. . . . It was very lightweight, like balsa wood. It wasn't a large piece, maybe about four inches long, maybe just a little larger than a pencil. We cut on it with a knife and would hold a match on it, and it wouldn't burn. We knew it wasn't wood. It was smooth like plastic. . . . I hadn't seen anything like it.

Brazel's daughter, Bessie Brazel Schreiber, testified several years after the fact that the material she saw was

> a sort of aluminum like foil. Some of [these] pieces had a sort of tape stuck to them. . . . It could not be peeled off or removed at all. Some of these pieces had something like numbers and lettering on them, but there were no words we were able to make out. The figures were written out like you would write numbers in columns . . . but they didn't look like the numbers we use at all.

Brazel and the boy scooped up several pieces of the strange material and put them in the truck to take home. Although he was disturbed by what he had found in the remote pasture, Brazel did not mention his discovery to anyone at first other than his and Dee's families and a few friends. Finally, however, one of his neighbors persuaded him to call the authorities. So on Sunday, July 6, Brazel drove into Corona and told Chaves County Sheriff George Wilcox the whole story. Wilcox, not knowing what to make of the situation, called Major Jesse Marcel, an intelligence officer at nearby Roswell Army Air Field.

Marcel and another intelligence officer made the trip out to the ranch and recovered a great amount of the strange-looking material, which rumor had it was from some sort of unidentified flying object. On July 8, the public information officer at Roswell, under the direction of the base commandant, issued a press release that stated:

> The many rumors regarding the flying disc became a reality yesterday when the Intelligence office of the 509th Bomb Group of the Eighth Air Force, Roswell Army Air Field, was fortunate enough to gain possession of a disc through the cooperation of one of the local residents and the sheriff's office of Chaves County.
>
> The flying object landed on a ranch near Roswell sometime last week. Not having phone facilities, the rancher stored the disc until such time as he was able to contact the sheriff's office, who in turn notified Major Jesse A. Marcel of the 509th Bomb Group Intelligence Office.

Action was immediately taken and the disc was picked up at the rancher's home. It was inspected at the Roswell Army Air Field and subsequently loaned by Major Marcel to higher headquarters.

Within three hours of the release of the above story, higher-ups within the U.S. Army retracted the news and issued a statement saying that the object was nothing more than a radar reflector from a lost weather balloon. An army team was sent to the Foster Ranch, where every piece of the mysterious material was picked up and taken back to the base at Roswell. Brazel was held by military authorities and interrogated for several days before finally being released. He never mentioned the bizarre incident again.

With the benefit of hindsight, it seems obvious that the federal government successfully covered up what may have been the first physical evidence of UFOs. The entire event was swept under the carpet as if it had never happened. Although the government set up several projects ostensibly to investigate unusual sightings and other aberrant phenomena, project leaders rarely took their tasks seriously. In the seventy-five years since, thousands of UFO sightings have been reported all over the world, none of which has ever been acknowledged as genuine by government officials.

1950

The Real Story of
Smokey Bear

Harlow Yeager, a Forest Service ranger, looked all about him at the smoldering remains of what had once been a vibrant, green wilderness paradise. As far as he could see in every direction were the blackened skeletons of tree trunks and the smoking corpses of small game animals that had failed to escape the massive forest fire's hot breath. Yeager was standing in the midst of New Mexico's Lincoln National Forest, and the ghastly scene he surveyed was the result of a large conflagration that over the past several days had burned seventeen thousand acres of prime ponderosa pine forestland.

As Yeager took one last look at the wasteland before him, his eye was attracted to something moving in the charred remains of a tree. When he walked closer, he discovered a tiny black bear cub hugging a burned-out pine trunk. Yeager carefully removed the squalling five-pound cub and checked him for burns. The little fellow's foot pads were singed from the intense heat of the burned tree, and he probably had not eaten for days. Otherwise he appeared to be in relatively good health. After calming the scared cub with soothing talk and a good petting, the ranger gave him to a member of his crew and instructed him to carry the animal back to camp where first aid could be administered.

It was late spring 1950, and so far this year, little rain had visited the conifer forests that clung to the slopes of the Capitan Mountains in south-central New Mexico. What little moisture had fallen had been quickly absorbed by the loose pine tinder that blanketed the forest floor. The area was a disaster waiting to happen, and on May 4, the awful tragedy struck.

Perhaps the culprit was a bolt of lightning, or maybe it was a careless camper. Regardless of the cause, flames flew like the wind through the dry forests, and before rangers could arrive, the fire was out of control. Local, state, and federal firefighters were reinforced by soldiers from the air base sixty miles away at Roswell and from Fort Bliss, Texas.

A potentially deadly situation arose when several soldiers were surrounded by the fire's intense flames. A rock pile provided an island on which the men hoped to escape the inferno. Each one laid down and placed a wet handkerchief over his face, hoping and praying that the fire would go around the rocks. The men lay there for almost an hour, and the flames finally passed. Miraculously all the men were unharmed.

Now the fire was under control, and the firefighters were slowly leaving the area. Back at camp, the little bear cub was causing considerable excitement. The men tried to feed him, but the animal was too frightened to eat. Finally Ross Flatley, who owned a nearby ranch, announced that he and his wife, Patricia, would care for the tiny cub until other arrangements could be made. Ray Bell, a New Mexico game warden, visited the ranch the following day and retrieved the bear. It was then that Bell conceived the idea of using the cub as the living emblem of a fire prevention program implemented by the Forest Service several years earlier. It had been utilizing an imaginary bear named "Smokey" as its "spokesman." Bell was encouraged when everyone he talked to thought the idea was a good one.

Bell flew the bear cub to a veterinarian in Santa Fe, who treated the burns on its paws. Six days later Bell's five-year-old daughter, Judy, persuaded her father to bring the cub home so that she and her mother could nurse it back to health.

Bell's boss was Elliott Barker, a legend among New Mexico outdoorsmen and conservationists. Barker, the director of the New Mexico Game and Fish Department, liked the idea of using a live bear to increase public awareness of the tragedy of forest fires. When he telephoned authorities in Washington, D.C., and laid the plan before them, they liked it as well. And so the orphan cub officially became "Smokey Bear." Excited Forest Service officials decided to fly Smokey to Washington and house him at the National Zoological Park. His job would be to act as "national spokesman" for the cause of forest-fire prevention.

After two commercial airlines refused to fly Smokey unless he was placed in the luggage compartment, Frank Hines, the owner of a flying service in Hobbs, New Mexico, volunteered his time and an airplane to take the cub to the nation's capital. A local artist was hired to paint a picture of Smokey on both sides of the plane's fuselage. On June 27, 1950, Smokey, accompanied by two local forest rangers, took off for Washington, D.C.

By now news of Smokey's remarkable rescue had spread across the country. At nearly every airport at which the plane stopped to refuel, crowds of curious onlookers gathered for a peek at the brave little bear. When the plane finally touched down in Washington, Smokey was on his way to becoming a national hero.

For twenty-six years Smokey Bear was the living symbol of a nation's pride in its forests and its dedication to fire prevention. An entire generation of children grew up seeing Smokey's friendly face and ever-present shovel and hearing his admonition that "only you can prevent forest fires." When Smokey died in November 1976, he was probably the best-known animal in the United States. His body was transported back to New Mexico and buried at Capitan, near Lincoln National Forest. The Capitan Ranger District, where the cub had been found, was renamed "Smokey Bear" in 1960. Later it combined with another district to become the present-day Smokey Bear Ranger District. Today Smokey Bear State Park commemorates the place of birth and burial of this lovable bear that became a legend in his own time.

1977

Operation Goldfinger

During the early morning hours of March 19, 1977, a strange spectacle appeared in the desert along the western border of the White Sands Missile Range in southern New Mexico. A convoy of nearly seventy all-terrain vehicles, carrying dozens of U.S. Army officials, newspaper reporters, photographers, scientists, professional treasure hunters, physicists, and other adventurers, made its way through the parched landscape toward a remote mountain in the San Andres Range. The cavalcade's destination was Victorio Peak in the middle of Hembrillo Basin. Named after the famous Apache chief, the peak was rumored to have several million dollars worth of gold buried beneath its five-hundred-foot-high basalt cone. The mission of the caravan that slowly snaked its way along the federally owned missile range was to determine once and for all whether the rumors were true.

"Operation Goldfinger," as the project was called, was authorized by the federal government after years of speculation about the existence of a massive, underground treasure trove that some thought might date back to the Spanish conquistadors. The gold was supposedly buried deep within Victorio Peak, amid a maze of underground caves. There were those who claimed to have seen some of the gold bars from this bonanza.

The legend of the lost Victorio Peak gold had originated in the late 1920s when, according to several old-timers in the area, gold bars began to show up in the neighborhood. Then, in 1935, Milton "Doc" Noss, an ex-convict who practiced podiatry, showed up in Hatch, New Mexico, a small village on the west bank of the Rio Grande, near the White Sands region. Noss and his wife, Ova, lived a quiet life in Hatch until one day in 1937, when they were hunting deer in the San Andres Mountains. They stumbled upon a shaft in Victorio Peak that Noss described as "big enough for a freight train and leading into small cave rooms along the side." As Noss groped through the semidarkness of the cavern with nothing but a flashlight to illuminate the way, he came across a human skeleton. He later described it as having "red hair and grinning up at me." Just beyond this harrowing discovery, Noss found twenty-six more skeletons.

According to David Leon Chandler, in his book, *100 Tons of Gold*, the twenty-seven skeletons were not all the bewildered Noss discovered.

In one of the smaller rooms, just beyond the skeletons, Doc found what he had half expected: treasure.

He saw old Wells Fargo chests, swords, guns, saddles, jewels, boxes full of old letters, and "enough gold and silver coins to load sixty to eighty mules."

Doc filled his pockets with coins and jewels and started happily out of the cave. Then—back near the shaft, in a corner of the main cave and covered with old buffalo hides—he found thousands upon thousands of bars of pig iron, "stacked like cordwood."

It was only after Noss had returned to the surface that his wife rubbed one of the "pig iron" bars and discovered that it was gold! The pair were delirious with joy. They had struck it rich, and no one else knew about their discovery.

"We knew we had something," Ova said later. "We knew it was ours." It was the "happiest moment in our lives."

Years later, in 1952, experts confirmed the quality and value of the gold bars in affidavits to Secretary of Defense Robert Lovett. One statement read:

I worked with Doc Noss to carry gold out of the mine. In 1939 I took one bullion bar to Douglas, Arizona, and had Holly and Holly assayers test it, and it assayed to run over $5,000 gold per ton. . . . The bar was a regular Wells Fargo gold bar. I saw quite a few other bars of the same type.

Sometime during 1939, Noss's worst nightmare came true. While attempting to enlarge the opening to the cave containing the gold, the rock caved in and completely blocked entry into the cavern. In 1958 several air force personnel apparently found another way into the treasure cave, but when Captain Leonard Fiege, the group's leader, returned to the site with his superiors, he couldn't find the entrance again.

In 1949 Noss was murdered in an incident unrelated to the gold, but his wife never stopped trying to relocate the cave. She suspected that the army was stealing her gold, so over the next several years, she sought government permission to try to find her late husband's treasure. Finally, after long and complex negotiations that involved even the eminent trial lawyer F. Lee Bailey, the army, still maintaining that there was no gold in Victorio Peak, consented to search the area. And so, in March 1977, Operation Goldfinger was launched.

Ova Noss was present as mining and army personnel searched for ten days in the vicinity of Victorio Peak. She and other spectators could see that the army had not only worked Noss's claim in years past, but they had even blasted several of the caves and erected giant iron doors to keep out all comers. The search for the gold turned up absolutely nothing. The army maintained that it had been right after all. Ova Noss accused the military of jumping her claim, stealing all the gold, and destroying the remains of the caves. To this date no one has located Doc Noss's gold.

1980

The Great Prison Riot

Americans will remember the year 1980 for several events that affected their lives in one way or another. From an economic standpoint, borrowers wringing their hands and savers applauded as the prime interest rate rose to an all-time high of 21.5 percent. Music lovers were deeply saddened when they learned that Beatles icon, John Lennon, was gunned down by a deranged follower outside his New York City apartment. And few will ever forget the terrifying drama of the eruption of Mount St. Helens, as it played out on live television. But there was another memorable event that year—one that occurred in New Mexico in early February and made national headlines, provoking a universal dialogue among the law enforcement, corrections, and legal communities.

As February 1980 arrived in Santa Fe, the temperatures averaged around forty degrees and weather forecasters were predicting up to ten inches of new snow for the ski slopes outside of town. The Sweeney Convention Center, at the corner of Marcy Street and Grant Avenue, was hosting a sold-out crowd for the Bach Festival, and people milled about the downtown streets in a festive mood. However, inmates at the Penitentiary of New Mexico, located ten miles south of town along Highway 14, had little reason to be merry, and rumors quickly circulated among them that an uprising was about to take place.

Twenty-four men were responsible for the prison's criminal population of nearly twelve hundred inmates. Just before midnight on February 1, the prison's captain of the guard and twenty-three guards prepared themselves for the graveyard shift they had pulled so many times before. Although the captain had heard from an informant that trouble might be brewing, he more or less brushed off the rumors as he and three assistants started on their rounds of the prison to take head counts, secure the day rooms, and lock the strong metal doors that separated the cell blocks.

In the meantime, several residents of Dormitory E-2, had, for the past several hours, been entertaining themselves by drinking enormous quantities of "Raisin Jack," a kind of prison-made moonshine distilled from sugar, raisins, yeast, and water and fermented for several days in plastic bags hidden in the air vents. By the time the captain and three guards made their way to the dormitory at around 1:40 a.m., on February 2, many of the inebriated inmates had already laid their plans for the uprising.

Upon entering Dormitory E-2, the four prison guards were attacked and overcome. One of the younger guards, putting up a fierce resistance, was repeatedly clubbed until his head was covered with blood. The inmates then stripped, handcuffed, and blindfolded the guards before storming out of the dormitory and proceeding to Dormitories E-1, F-1, and A-2, where other hostages were taken.

By now the instigators of the riot had made their way down several corridors, opening cell door after cell door and freeing hundreds of prisoners. Within twenty-two minutes of the inmates' taking of Dormitory E-2, they had overcome the control center, a strongly fortified room containing the keys to most of the prison's doors, including those to the armory and the warden's office, wherein were housed inmate records. Several hours later prisoners began a search of the warden's files to identify names of their cohorts who had collaborated with authorities. Before the reign of terror was over, many of these "snitch" inmates would die, some so violently as to defy description, at the hands of fellow prisoners.

As the morning of February 2 wore on, the violent inmates continued their mission of murder, mayhem, and destruction. They entered the prison's hospital and raided its drugs and narcotics inventories. More hostages from both the prison population and the guard staff were taken. The doors to the notorious Cellblock 3, wherein the most incorrigible inmates were housed, were opened and more prisoners fled into the corridors. By 7:00 a.m., several terrified prisoners had been hustled out of Cellblock 4, the home to the penitentiary's protective custody inmates. Fires were started in the chapel and the warden's office, as inmates watched Dormitories B-1 and B-2 go up in flames as well.

Units of the New Mexico state police and the National Guard arrived at the scene at around dawn on February 2, but for hours no effort was made to retake the prison for fear of more bloodshed, particularly among the hostages. Negotiations between state officials and inmate leaders began later in the day, with the prisoners making eleven basic demands, most having to do with overcrowding, poor food, and availability of educational facilities.

The hostages were eventually released and, miraculously, all twelve of the captured guards survived, although several of them were brutally and permanently wounded. At around 1:30 p.m., on February 3, state police and national guardsmen entered the prison complex and occupied it without firing a shot.

The effects of the riot were gruesome. Besides wounding and torturing the twelve prison guards, angry inmates murdered thirty-three of their fellow prisoners and wounded and mutilated many more. In all, ninety inmates were hospitalized for either wounds sustained in the riot or for drug overdoses following the raids on the prison hospital. The prison complex sustained more than one hundred million dollars' worth of damage. Built in 1956 as a state-of-the-art facility at a cost of eight million dollars, it was eventually replaced in 1997. Today New Mexico maintains a number of regional correctional facilities, some of them operated privately and some by the state.

The enormity of the economic effect, as well as the loss of life during New Mexico's tragic prison riot makes it one of the worst such occurrences in United States history.

1996

Greer Garson's Legacy

When the renowned Academy Award–winning actress Greer Garson arrived in New Mexico in 1949 to join her new husband, E. E. "Buddy" Fogelson, on his ranch near Pecos, she immediately fell in love with the vast, uncluttered spaces of north-central New Mexico. British-born Garson, best known at the time for her 1942 Oscar-winning role opposite Walter Pidgeon in *Mrs. Miniver*, was acting on the London stage in 1937 when she was discovered by Hollywood mogul Louis B. Mayer. Searching for a potential replacement for the soon-to-be retiring Greta Garbo and Norma Shearer, he was smitten by Garson's stunning beauty and immediately offered her a contract with MGM. Garson's first American movie was *Goodbye, Mr. Chips*, which garnered her an Academy Award nomination, a prize taken instead by Vivien

Leigh for her portrayal of Scarlett O'Hara in *Gone with the Wind*. By the time she moved to Forked Lightning Ranch, Garson had starred in sixteen American movies, and for six she had been nominated for an Oscar.

Fogelson was a wealthy Texas lawyer, geologist, rancher, oilman, and former colonel on General Dwight D. Eisenhower's staff during World War II. He had owned the Forked Lightning Ranch since 1941. He had purchased the fifty-five-hundred-acre spread from W. C. Currier, who in turn had acquired it five years earlier from "Tex" Austin. Austin, whose real name was Clarence Van Nostrand, was an adventurer and entrepreneur who, among other feats, had produced the first rodeo held in New York City's Madison Square Garden in 1922. He had hired a local fledgling architect, John Gaw Meem, to design and build the main ranch house, which overlooked the Pecos River. Meem later became internationally famous for the establishment of the "Pueblo Revival" style of architecture.

Although the Fogelsons also maintained homes in Dallas and Los Angeles, they were enamored by their New Mexico hideaway, where they could retreat from the pressures of their active and demanding careers. Fogelson gradually increased his holdings to thirteen thousand acres and introduced Santa Gertrudis cattle to the high elevations of northern New Mexico. The Santa Gertrudis breed, a cross between shorthorns and Brahmas, was developed on the famous King Ranch to better tolerate the hot, humid conditions of southeastern Texas. It was through Fogelson's untiring promotion of the strain that he proved it could tolerate the cooler climes of New Mexico as well.

The Forked Lightning Ranch stretched on both sides of the Pecos River between the present-day villages of Rowe and Pecos. From its source as a freshet high in the southern reaches of the Sangre de Cristo Mountains, the river eventually joins the Rio Grande faraway in Texas. The surrounding region represents a loosely defined boundary separating the Great Plains to the east and the drier highlands of New Mexico to the west.

Just as alluring as the geography and terrain of the area is its history. Nearby are the ruins of Pecos Pueblo, a complex of prehistoric ruins that also houses the remains of early Spanish missions. Coronado stopped by the pueblo in 1541 on his way to search out the fabled land of Quivira, and American teamsters took refuge within its decaying walls as they plied their trade along the Santa Fe Trail in the early to mid-nineteenth century. General Stephen Watts Kearny and his fabled Army of the West crossed the river nearby on their mission to occupy Santa Fe during the Mexican-American War in 1846. And during the Civil War, federal troops forever dashed Confederate hopes of an occupied New Mexico at Glorieta Pass a few miles westward.

Over the years the Fogelsons intermittently visited the ranch while both pursued their careers in Texas and Hollywood. Although they were not yet permanent residents, they always actively participated in community and charitable affairs in Santa Fe. In 1965 the couple funded what became the Greer Garson Theater at the College of Santa Fe. Later Buddy's munificence brought him the honor of having the college name the E. E. Fogelson Library in his honor, and Garson was awarded an honorary doctorate that she esteemed even more than all of her hard-earned Hollywood recognition. The couple were also staunch supporters of the Santa Fe Opera.

When the Pecos Pueblo and Spanish mission ruins were designated a national monument in the mid-1960s, fulfilling a longtime dream of the Fogelsons to extend federal protection to the fragile but extremely important archaeological site, they donated 279 acres of their beloved ranch to the federal government to be added to the sixty-two acres of existing ruins. In 1979 they donated an additional twenty-three acres, which contained a separate archaeological site. Two years later the U.S. Department of the Interior rewarded the Fogelsons with its highest honor, the Conservation Service Award.

By the late 1960s, the Fogelsons had more or less retired to their New Mexico ranch. Garson suffered a stroke in 1980, and two years later Buddy was diagnosed with Parkinson's disease. As the years passed and the couple's health continued to deteriorate, they moved to their Dallas home, where Buddy died in December 1987, leaving much of Forked Lightning Ranch to Garson. Earlier in the year New Mexico Governor Garry Caruthers had bestowed Garson with the prestigious Governor's Award for Excellence and Achievement in the Arts.

In 1988, when President Ronald Reagan was asked to contribute to a book being published about Pecos entitled *Pecos: Gateway to Pueblo & Plains,* he wrote that the volume "would tell Americans and visitors to our land a great deal about the fascinating history and heritage of the Pecos area, the American Southwest, and the Great Plains." He added,

> This trove of fact and lore is brought closer to us by
> ... the vision, the public spirit, and the determination of the late Colonel Buddy Fogelson and his wife Greer Garson Fogelson, who helped make the Pecos National Monument a reality and a lasting legacy.

May everyone who contemplates the Pecos and its rich meaning do so in their spirit. . . .

In 1990 Garson terminated negotiations to sell the ranch to developers when she learned that the company planned to build a resort community on the nearly six-thousand-acre spread remaining in her possession. The same year, Senators Jeff Bingaman and Pete Domenici and Representative Bill Richardson introduced legislation in both houses of Congress that would preserve the ranch as part of the newly recommended Pecos National Historical Park. The following year Greer sold Forked Lightning to the Conservation Fund, which, in turn, donated the property to the National Park Service.

Greer Garson Fogelson died of heart failure in Dallas on April 6, 1996, at the age of ninety-two. At the Academy Awards presentation the following year, she was honored with a memorial tribute. Only three other actresses have ever been nominated for an Oscar more times than Garson's seven: Katharine Hepburn, Bette Davis, and Geraldine Page.

NEW MEXICO FACTS AND TRIVIA

New Mexico is the fifth largest state in the nation after Alaska, Texas, California, and Montana. It encompasses 121,593 square miles, or almost seventy-eight million acres. Its greatest width, from east to west, is 350 miles, and its greatest length, north to south, is 390 miles.

The name New Mexico comes from the Spanish word *nuevo*, meaning "new," and the Aztec word *mexico*, meaning "place of [the god] Mexitli."

The mean elevation of New Mexico is 5,700 feet. The highest point in the state is Wheeler Peak, in Taos County, with an altitude of 13,161 feet. The lowest point (2,817 feet) is near the Texas border in Eddy County.

The geographical center of New Mexico is in Torrance County, twelve miles south-southwest of Willard.

The population of New Mexico in 2020 was 2.12 million.

The coldest temperature ever recorded in New Mexico was fifty degrees below zero Fahrenheit on February 1, 1951, at Gavilan.

The hottest temperature was 122 degrees Fahrenheit on June 27, 1994, at Waste Isolation Pilot Pit.

New Mexico became a U.S. territory on May 25, 1850. It became the forty-seventh state on January 6, 1912.

Santa Fe is the capital of New Mexico. Its estimated population in 2010 was 70,631. Albuquerque is the state's largest city, with an estimated population in 2010 of 545,852.

New Mexico contains thirty-three counties.

The state motto, adopted in 1913, is *Crescit Eundo*, or "It Grows As It Goes."

New Mexico's official nickname is "Land of Enchantment." It is also known as "the Sunshine State" and "the Cactus State."

The state bird, adopted in 1949, is the roadrunner, *Geococcyx californianus*. Called the "cuckoo that runs on the ground," the slender bird is twenty to twenty-four inches long and lives in the dry open country that characterizes much of the state.

The state mammal, adopted in 1963, is the black bear, *Ursus americanus*. At one time the inquisitive black bear was native to all forty-eight contiguous states. It is still fairly common in the wilder sections of New Mexico.

The state flower, adopted in 1927, is the yucca, *Yucca glauca*, a common desert plant. Many Native tribes found the yucca plant useful in the manufacture of cord, brushes, and soap.

The state songs, adopted in 1917 and 1971 respectively, are "O Fair New Mexico" and "Asi es Nuevo Mexico."

The state fish, adopted in 1955, is the cutthroat trout, *Salmo clarkii*. Native in rapid flowing streams throughout the higher elevations of the Rocky Mountain region, the cutthroat is distinguished by the red markings below its gill covers.

The state tree, adopted in 1949, is the piñon pine, *Pinus edulis*. This small pine grows at altitudes of five thousand to eight thousand feet throughout much of New Mexico's rugged canyon country. Its sweet-tasting nuts are eaten by a variety of birds and animals. At one time they were an important part of the diets of indigenous people as well.

The state gem, adopted in 1967, is turquoise. The beautiful blue, blue-green, and green stones occur naturally in many locales in New Mexico. Although the Pueblo Natives have made turquoise jewelry since prehistoric times, the gem reached its height of popularity in the United States after Navajo Natives learned to work with silver in the mid-nineteenth century, combining the two natural elements into exquisite jewelry.

The state vegetables, adopted in 1965, are the chili pepper and the pinto bean, important components of the ever-popular New Mexican food.

The state flag, adopted in 1925, consists of a red stylized sun (the zia symbol of the ancient Zia Pueblo Natives) on a yellow field.

New Mexico's state seal consists of two eagles poised above a scroll bearing the state motto.

BIBLIOGRAPHY

Books

Askins, Colonel Charles. "The .45 Auto with Pershing in Mexico." In *America: The Men and Their Guns That Made Her Great*, edited by Charles Boddington. Los Angeles: Petersen Publishing Company, 1981.

Beachum, Larry M. *William Becknell: Father of the Santa Fe Trade*. El Paso: Texas Western Press, 1982.

Briggs, Walter. *Without Noise of Arms*. Flagstaff, Arizona: Northland Press, 1976.

Bryan, Howard. *Wildest of the Wild West*. Santa Fe: Clear Light Publishers, 1988.

Chandler, David Leon. *100 Tons of Gold*. New York: Doubleday and Company, 1978.

Conant, Jennet. *109 East Palace: Robert Oppenheimer and the Secret City of Los Alamos*. New York: Simon & Schuster, 2005.

Crutchfield, James A. *Tragedy at Taos: The Revolt of 1847*. Plano, Texas: The Republic of Texas Press, 1995.

Crutchfield, James A. *Revolt at Taos: The New Mexican and Indian Insurrection of 1847*. Yardley, PA: Westholme Publishing, 2015.

Day, A. Grove. *Coronado's Quest: The Discovery of the Southwestern States*. Berkeley: University of California Press, 1964.

Evans, Max. *Long John Dunn of Taos: From Texas Outlaw to New Mexico Hero*. Santa Fe: Clear Light Publishers, 1993.

Folsom, Franklin. *Black Cowboy: The Life and Legend of George McJunkin*. Niwot, Colorado: Robert Rinehart Publishers, 1992.

Forrest, Earl R. *Missions and Pueblos of the Old Southwest*. Chicago: Rio Grande Press, 1965.

Friedman, Stanton T., and Don Berliner. *Crash at Corona*. New York: Paragon House, 1992.

Garrett, Pat. *The Authentic Life of Billy, the Kid*. Norman: University of Oklahoma Press, 1954.

Hodel, Donald P. "Introduction." In *Pecos: Gateway to Pueblos and Plains*, edited by John V. Bezy and Joseph P. Sanchez. Tucson: Southwest Parks and Monuments Association, 1988.

Horan, James D. *Pictorial History of the Wild West*. New York: Crown Publishers, 1954.

Horgan, Paul. *Great River: The Rio Grande in North American History, Volume 2*. New York: Rinehart and Company, 1954.

Josephy, Alvin J. *War on the Frontier: The Trans-Mississippi West*. Alexandria, Virginia: Time-Life Books, 1986.

Kendall, George Wilkins. *Narrative of the Texan Santa Fe Expedition*. New York: Harper and Brothers, 1844.

Leckie, William H. *The Buffalo Soldiers*. Norman: University of Oklahoma Press, 1967.

Meriwether, David. *My Life in the Mountains and on the Plains*. Norman: University of Oklahoma Press, 1965.

Methvin, Reverend J. J. *Andele, or the Mexican-Kiowa Captive*. Louisville, Kentucky: Pentecostal Herald Press, 1899.

Metz, Leon C. *The Shooters*. El Paso: Mangan Books, 1976.

Meyer, Marian. *Mary Donoho, New First Lady of the Santa Fe Trail*. Santa Fe: Ancient City Press, 1991.

Nolan, Frederick. *The Lincoln County War: A Documentary History*. Norman: University of Oklahoma Press, 1992.

Pike, Zebulon. *An Account of Expeditions to the Sources of the Mississippi, and through the Western Parts of Louisiana, to the Sources of the Arkansaw, Kans, La Platte, and Pierre Jaun Rivers.* Philadelphia: C. and A. Conrad and Company, 1810.

Reedstrom, E. Lisle. *Apache Wars: An Illustrated Battle History.* New York: Sterling Publishing Company, 1990.

Rhodes, Richard. *The Making of the Atomic Bomb.* New York: Simon and Schuster, 1986.

Saenz, Adolph. *Politics of a Prison Riot: The 1980 New Mexico Prison Riot: Its Causes and Aftermath.* Corrales, NM: Rhombus Publishing Company, 1986.

Samuels, Peggy and Harold. *Samuels' Encyclopedia of Artists of the American West.* Secaucus, New Jersey: Castle Books, 1985.

Sanchez, Joseph P. "Cicuye and the First Spaniards." In *Pecos: Gateway to Pueblos and Plains,* edited by John V. Bezy and Joseph P. Sanchez. Tucson: Southwest Parks and Monuments Association, 1988.

———. "The Peralta-Ordonez Affair and the Founding of Santa Fe." In *Santa Fe: History of an Ancient City,* edited by David Grant Noble. Santa Fe: School of American Research Press, 1989.

Seton, Ernest Thompson. *Trail of an Artist Naturalist.* New York: Charles Scribner's Sons, 1948.

Sherman, John. *Taos: A Pictorial History.* Santa Fe: William Gannon, 1990.

Silva, Lee A. "Elfego Baca: Forgotten Fighter for Law and Order." In *America: The Men and Their Guns That Made Her Great,* edited by Craig Boddington. Los Angeles: Petersen Publishing Company, 1981.

Thrapp, Dan L. *Encyclopedia of Frontier Biography.* Glendale, California: The Arthur H. Clark Company, 1988.

Weber, David J. *The Spanish Frontier in North America.* New Haven: Yale University Press, 1992.

Other Sources

McDonald, Russ. "Bandit Robs Train Once Too Often," *The National Tombstone Epitaph,* July 1991.

Utley, Robert M. "Report on the Integrity of Glorieta Pass Battlefield, New Mexico." U.S. Department of the Interior, National Park Service, no date.

Watkins, T. H. "The Brotherhood of the Mountains," *American Heritage*, Volume 30, Number 3.

Westermeier, Clifford P. "Teddy's Terrors: The New Mexican Volunteers of 1898," *New Mexico Historical Review*, Volume 27.

Wolff, Leon. "Black Jack's Mexican Goose Chase," *American Heritage*, Volume 13, Number 4.

INDEX

Rhodes, Richard, 119
Richardson, Representative Bill, 141
Richmond, Virginia, 55
Rio Arriba County, 115
Rio Chama, 21
Rio Grande, 15, 16, 20, 24, 80, 81, 86, 130, 139
Rio Grande Railroad, 81
roadrunner, 143
Roosevelt, President Franklin D., 119
Roosevelt, Theodore, 92–95, 103
Roswell Army Air Field, x, 121–24, 126
Rough Riders, 91–95, 103
Rowe, New Mexico, 138
Ruxton, George, 49–50

S

Saint Louis, Missouri, 24, 34, 91
Saint Vrain, Ceran, 45
San Andres Mountains, 118, 129, 130
San Antonio, Texas, 94, 103
San Carlos Reservation, 65
San Gabriel, 12
San Ildefonso Pueblo, 20
San Juan Heights, Cuba, 94
San Juan, New Mexico, 15
San Juan River, x, 21
San Miguel County, 39
San Miguel, New Mexico, 33, 35, 37, 41, 115
Sangre de Cristo Mountains, 79, 88, 116, 139
Santa Clara Pueblo, 20–21
Santa Fe Gazette, 30
Santa Fe New Mexican, 92–93
Santa Fe, New Mexico, x, 11–17, 19–24, 27–34, 41–42, 44, 47, 51, 53, 55, 72, 86, 91, 98, 109, 127, 134, 139, 143
Santa Fe Opera, 139
Santa Fe Trail, 33–36, 39, 53, 116

Santa Gertrudis cattle, 138
Santo Domingo Pueblo, 11–13
Sarracino, Deputy Sheriff Pedro, 74–76
Schreiber, Bessie Brazel, 122
Schwachheim, Carl, 4
Scurry, Lieutenant Colonel W. F., 53–55
Seton Castle, 86
Seton, Ernest Thompson, 83–86
Sharp, Joseph, 88–89
Sheldon, Lionel A., 72
Sibley, General Henry Hopkins, 52–56
Slaughter, John B., 76
Slocum, Colonel H. J., 104
Slough, Colonel John P., 54
Smokey Bear, 125–28
Smokey Bear Ranger District, 128
Smokey Bear State Park, 128
Socorro, New Mexico, x, 74, 76, 77
Spain, 8, 20–27, 30, 32, 92, 94
    expansion into America, 6–22
Spanish–American War, 24, 89
Sweeney Convention Center, 134

T

Taos County, 16, 142
Taos Foundation, 112
Taos Natives, 45, 47, 49
Taos Lightning, 48
Taos, New Mexico, x, 43, 44, 46, 48–51, 79–82, 87–90. 108–112, 115
    art colony, 82, 87–90
Taos News, 108
Taos Pueblo, 15, 47, 51
Taos Society of Artists, 90, 112
Teller, Edward, 118
Tesuque Pueblo, 20
Tewa Natives, 15, 20
Texan Santa Fe Expedition, 35–38
Texas Mounted Volunteers, 52, 53

ABOUT THE AUTHOR

During his five-decade-long writing career, **James A. Crutchfield** has published nearly seventy books pertaining to United States history and biography. His articles have appeared in magazines, newspapers, and journals across the country, earning multiple awards from Library Journal, the Daughters of the American Revolution, the American Association for State and Local History, and Western Writers of America. In 2011, Western Writers of America presented him with the Owen Wister Award for Lifetime Achievement in Western History and Literature. In 2015, Crutchfield was inducted into the Western Writers Hall of Fame housed in the McCracken Research Library at the Buffalo Bill Center of the West in Cody, Wyoming. He lives in Tennessee with his wife, Regena, and their cat, Sir Oliver Crutchfield, OBE.